VOLUNTEERING
With Your Pet

How to Get Involved in Animal-Assisted Therapy With Any Kind of Pet

By Mary R. Burch, PhD

HOWELL
BOOK
HOUSE

Macmillan • USA

Howell Book House

A Simon & Schuster Macmillan Company

1633 Broadway

New York, NY 10019-6785

Library of Congress Cataloging-in-Publication Data

Burch, Mary R.

    Volunteering with your pet : how to get involved in animal-assisted therapy with any kind of pet / by Mary R. Burch.

    p. cm.

ISBN 0-87605-791-1

Book design by Kris Tobiassen

    1. Pets—Therapeutic use. I. Title.

RM931.A65B87 1996

615.8'515—dc20   95-38944

    CIP

For My Dad
He taught me that animals were important
members of a family

CONTENTS

FOREWORD

Dr. Mary Burch's *Volunteering With Your Pet* is a necessary manual for anyone who wishes to join the growing number of volunteers who are bringing comfort and well-being into therapy settings by supplementing conventional medicine with the healing potential of contact with animals.

Presently, we are able to assess both the enormous gains and limitations of technological medicine. The reassessment of the value of many older and widely distributed ways of healing is occurring simultaneously with the growing awareness that we will have to learn how to live more harmoniously with the natural world that spawned us, and preserve it as a home for us and our children. Just as we are becoming aware of the necessity of preserving seas, wilderness and forest for the integrity of our globe, we are also recognizing that four and one-half million years of evolution have made us dependent upon contact with the animals and green life around us.

There is more and more evidence that human beings cannot reach their fullest potential unless they remain in contact with the natural world through companion animals, parks, gardens, farms and wilderness. Careful scientific investigation has documented the benefits of contact with companion animals and nature. For example, patients with heart disease have a better chance of survival if they have pets; contact with pets or the sights and sounds of nature lower blood pressure and reduce stress; older people with pets require fewer doctor visits; and patients who have a view of a park use less medication and are discharged earlier than patients who don't.

Investigation of the effects of companion animals and nature on our health and well-being progressed in parallel with increasing use of animals therapeutically with a wide variety of patients, but especially those abandoned by technological medicine: inmates of facilities for the aged, including those with Alzheimer's disease; chronic mental patients; children with autism or cerebral palsy; and patients with severe injuries requiring long and difficult rehabilitation. All of these people find themselves shut away from society, and vulnerable to the effects of institutionalization, which include withdrawal, depression and apathy. The very simple act of permitting them contact with companion animals and their owners can make a real, positive and therapeutic difference in their lives.

Certainly, we know that therapeutic contact with animals is worthwhile, but anything worthwhile doing must be done well. *Volunteering With Your Pet* will permit potential volunteers to do their best with minute particulars.

If animal-assisted therapy can provide real benefits to patients, why should it be a volunteer activity instead of being administered by professionals like doctors, psychologists, nurses or recreational therapists? The answer is quite simple. With the health care budget under such intense attack, resources will have to be devoted to technological medicine. With our current social priorities, we will not be able to afford many of the kinds of therapeutic encounters that would benefit the chronically ill and the chronically institutionalized.

We will always need volunteers to talk to patients, bring their animals to see patients, help patients maintain indoor plants and gardens, fish tanks and terrariums, and take them on outings to parks and gardens. All of these contacts heal and increase the quality of life. For some they may be the difference between recovery and persistent immobility and apathy. Yet our society will most likely remain dependent upon volunteers to bring these gifts of life into hospitals and chronic care institutions. Perhaps that is as it should be, because in joining people and nature we assert a common bond that benefits all: volunteer, patient and animal.

This is the only book for volunteers I know of that provides a full picture of the demands and the opportunities in animal-assisted therapy and activities. Dr. Burch gives a social guide that directs the volunteers to organizations that can help them to find facility affiliations, support, sources of new information, as well as training and certification and insurance. The book properly suggests that the volunteer is also a professional—just an unpaid one—who has an obligation to master the knowledge which will make his/her efforts effective and safe. That kind of pursuit requires both the support and information that an organization can bring. Like a professional, Dr. Burch also orients the volunteer for his/her responsibility to maintain the integrity of the process—even when that responsibility may conflict with institutional goals.

There are two ways to think about animal-assisted therapy. One focuses on the social and emotional relationships between animal, handler, patient and staff. The significance and effectiveness of the event is explained by the capacity of animals to evoke social inter-action, dialogue and emotion. The therapist guides the interaction trying to evoke responses, interact with the patient, and construct the kinds of tasks that the patient can learn rapidly, improving his feelings of competence.

The other way to conceptualize the event, which is not at all incompatible with the first, is to think of the animal as a powerful reward, not unlike any other kind of reward which can shape the patient's behavior in desired directions. Dr. Burch provides a masterful presentation of this second way of proceeding, which needs to be more precisely structured than the first, but, of course, relies on the same attraction that the animal provides.

Just as the first is free-flowing and catch-as-catch-can, filled with play and the unexpected, the second is precise, demanding careful statement of sequential goals. The first can be the province of the volunteer alone, but the second requires the cooperation of a trained diagnostician and therapist to analyze the behavior and set the goals. Dr. Burch does a great service to the field by presenting both of these complementary methods, introducing the volunteer to two opportunities, one allowing independence and one requiring the close cooperation of a trained professional. The volunteer can be a change agent in the therapy environment by recognizing the power of an animal to influence behavior—and suggesting that the therapists incorporate animal contact into their behavior modification regimen or program.

Dr. Burch's informed intelligence is guided by a deep love for animals and the people who need them. This commitment shines out of the text and the illustrations. The book is particularly illuminated by Dr. Burch's loving description of her father's terminal illness and the role that animals, wild and tame, played in bringing some pleasure and peace into those difficult days. Sharing that experience suggests that the care we give others and the care we give animals are both part of a larger whole in which all life is united and care given is care received.

Aaron Katcher, MD
Associate Professor Emeritus
Oral Medicine and Psychiatry
University of Pennsylvania

ACKNOWLEDGMENTS

As a person who is trained in behavioral science, I understand that a little reinforcement at the right time can go a long way. This is true when you are training an animal or working with people. I was lucky when it came to animal-assisted therapy; at all the critical times, I had somebody give me just the praise or encouragement I needed.

In 1985, I was attending a psychology conference in New York City. As an enthusiastic new convert to dog obedience training, I decided to take a break from the conference to visit the American Kennel Club. I wandered into the office of Jim Dearinger who was, at the time, the Director of Obedience. I told Jim about my background, interests and professional training, and his one-sentence response motivated me and guided how I chose to spend most of my time for the next several years. He said, "You've got the ability to make a contribution, you better get at it."

My work in the animal-assisted therapy world would not have been possible had it not been for Laddie, my first therapy dog. Laddie would not have been a therapy dog if we had not met Duane Pickel, our friend and obedience trainer. Duane has the ability to train any breed of dog. More amazing than that, he is unique in that he can also take any uncoordinated handler with any messed-up dog and teach the person to train the dog.

As an animal-assisted therapist, I am grateful to the Delta Society for providing me with professional development in this area that no other group offered when I was beginning my work in this field. In addition to competency-based training and opportunities to participate in stimulating, challenging activities, Delta provided me with a supporting network of colleagues who could always be counted on to answer questions or give advice.

Finally, I am indebted to Jon Bailey. When my 14-year-old Siberian Husky, Hauser, died, he recognized my signs of clinical depression and insisted that I get Laddie. He said, "I've figured it out. There are some people in this world who need a dog in order to live. I think you're one of those people."

INTRODUCTION

Why Do It?

Do you love your pet? Do you like spending time with your pet? Do you like introducing your pet to other people? Are you a person who would like to help others? If the answer to each of these questions is yes, then you may want to consider volunteering with your pet.

This book will tell you about the rich history of the field of animal-assisted therapy. You will learn practical information pertaining to how you can go about having your pet screened for therapy work and how you can get involved in volunteering in an animal-assisted therapy setting.

Trained as a behavior analyst, I started using animals in therapy about ten years ago. I got involved in this field quite by accident, and I have to admit that my initial intentions were not entirely honorable. I was looking for any distraction that could make my dog more steady in the obedience ring. One day, I saw an ad in the paper that said volunteers and dogs were needed for an animal-assisted therapy program. "Great," I thought, "there will be plenty of distractions in the halls of a nursing home." On our first visit, we had a nice time, but it still didn't dawn on me that I would ever use my dog in therapy sessions with my own clients. The idea first came to Laddie, who was my dog. On our third visit, we were introduced to Esther, an older woman who had the advanced stages of Alzheimer's disease. Appearing like a profoundly retarded woman, she repeated, "na-na-na-na."

A variety of animals can be used for therapy programs.
Delta Society

"Hi, I'm Mary. How are you?" I asked. "Na-na-na-na," was Esther's response. But when she saw Laddie, something happened. "What a nice dog," she said. "Come here, honey. Lie down and take a nap." I knew then that I was witnessing something powerful. For Esther, there was apparently some repertoire of nurturing that was still intact. The dog triggered a response that I was unable to elicit. On that day, I became a believer in animal-assisted therapy for the right reasons.

Animal-assisted therapy is a field that is growing by leaps and bounds. In the last twenty years there have been tremendous advances in animal-assisted therapy work and there are currently programs for volunteers in almost every setting imaginable. These settings include hospitals, nursing homes, schools, hospices, prisons and facilities for people who are developmentally disabled.

All kinds of animals participate in animal-assisted therapy programs. Dogs, cats, horses, rabbits, guinea pigs, birds and farm animals can all be suitable for therapy programs.

If you love your pet and would like to share it with others, volunteering with your pet is something that you may want to consider. With the proper screening and training, you and your pet can make a difference.

PART I

What It Involves

CHAPTER 1

A History of Animal-Assisted Therapy

If you are considering getting involved in animal-assisted therapy, be aware that you're about to become a part of a field with a very rich tradition. Pictures of doglike figures on cave walls suggest that animal-assisted therapy may have started when early man brought wolf cubs into the den to serve as companions for family members.

DOCUMENTED ACROSS THE CENTURIES

As early as 900 B.C., Homer wrote about Asklepios, the Greek god of healing. Asklepios had a divine healing power that was extended through sacred dogs and it was believed that a person who was blind could see immediately after being licked by a sacred dog. In ancient times, if a person was worried about going insane, he would carry a dog to prevent this from happening.

One of the first recorded therapeutic programs involving animals was started in the ninth century in Gheel, Belgium. Gheel is a farming area where many of the town's residents provide extended family care to people with disabilities. This is an animal-assisted therapy program that has stood the test of time. Even

3

In Gheel, Belgium, animals have been used in therapy settings since the ninth century.

today, caring for farm animals is a major component of the treatment program.

Another early, well documented animal-assisted therapy program was the York Retreat in Yorkshire, England. This program was founded in the 1790s by the Society of Friends. Rather than receive the traditional treatment of the times, which involved physical restraint and harsh drugs, patients at the York Retreat learned to care for animals and work in the garden.

Historically, the important role that animals can play in therapy has been noted in some nursing settings. In 1859, Florence Nightingale said, "A small pet animal is often an excellent companion for the sick. . . ."

ANIMALS IN THERAPY IN RECENT HISTORY

In the United States, as early as 1919, animals were used in St. Elizabeth's Hospital in Washington, D.C., for men in a mental health program. The visits at St. Elizabeth's continue today.

In the 1940s, the Red Cross worked at Army Air Corps hospitals with patients who were recovering from war injuries. Patients were permitted to work at the hospital's farm in order to keep their minds off the war.

In the 1950s, advances in animal-assisted therapy were made in the clinical psychology area. At Yeshiva University in New York, Dr. Borris Levinson found when his dog, Jingles, attended therapy sessions, he was able to make significant progress with a disturbed child. He continued to use the dog in treatment sessions and found that many children who were withdrawn and uncommunicative would interact positively with the dog. Levinson wrote a book about the potential of "pet-oriented child psychotherapy" and started a trend toward documentation and research in animal-assisted therapy.

Levinson seemed to have some vision about how much the field would grow and he encouraged the development of standards for both humans and animals who participated in animal-assisted therapy.

Dogs are popular teachers in schools, as the author and her dog demonstrate.

In the 1970s, the use of animals in therapy was expanded into other areas. In 1975, one of the most successful prison-based programs was started in Lima, Ohio. Small farm animals were used in the program, and research showed that inmates with pets to care for were less violent, had fewer infractions and less drug abuse, and needed less medication than those without pets.

Similar results were seen at the Purdy Women's Correction Center, a maximum security prison for women. At the Purdy program, inmates learned functional vocational skills such as dog care and grooming. The inmates were also trained as dog trainers and, for several years, service dogs were trained at the Purdy prgram. One of the first seizure detection dogs in the country received basic obedience training at Purdy. Sheba, a German Shepherd, could detect when her fourteen-year-old owner was going to have a seizure before it happened. As with all seizure detection dogs, Sheba's abilities to detect seizures were natural, untrained abilities.

In the early 1980s, animal-assisted therapy began to be noticed by the popular press. Dr. Aaron Katcher and his colleagues at the University of Pennsylvania made national news when they demonstrated in a controlled study that physical contact with an animal can lower the blood pressure in individuals with hypertension. Also along the lines of this research were studies of survivors of heart attacks that showed that more pet owners were alive after one year than non–pet owners.

Animals are currently used in every type of therapeutic setting you could think of, including nursing homes, developmental disabilities facilities and educational programs for people with physical disabilities and individuals with head injuries. They're used in therapy sessions for children who have been sexually or physically abused, in hospitals and hospices for AIDS and other terminally ill patients and in prisons and schools.

The most common settings for volunteers to visit are nursing homes. Many older people who are nursing-home residents will happily take a dog for a walk while they may refuse to go on an exercise walk that has been prescribed by a professional.

People with disabilities can be taught so many skills by using animals. They can learn specific skills about breeds and characteristics and how to care for an animal, as well as more general skills like responsibility.

In a number of programs around the country, dogs are used on hospital wards for terminally ill patients. There is some research that suggests that when we pet an animal, endorphins are released in our brains. Endorphins are the body's natural pain suppressers, and when some patients pet animals, they report less pain than when the animal is not present.

In so many settings, animals can provide great therapy; they give us unconditional love and acceptance. One day in the future, doctors might write out a new kind of prescription: "Spend more time hugging your pet."

WHAT'S IT REALLY CALLED?

You may have heard several different terms for this field, including "pet therapy," "pet-facilitated therapy" and "animal-assisted therapy." What should you call it?

Beginning in the 1980s, professionals that use animals in therapeutic settings began to make some distinctions about terminology. As the standards and levels of professionalism increased for the field, the terms "pet-facilitated therapy" and "pet therapy" began to be abandoned in favor of terms that did not suggest that simply any "pet" could perform therapy work. Even though you may volunteer with an animal that is your pet, by the time you get placed in a therapy setting, your "pet" will be different from the average pet in that it will have passed a screening and it will have achieved a basic level of training. Another reason professionals no longer use the term "pet therapy" is because it is used to describe what animal behaviorists do when they work with problem animals.

The most widely accepted terms for this field are currently "animal-assisted therapy," also known as AAT, and "animal-assisted activities," or AAA.

Animal-assisted therapy (AAT) involves working with clients when a specific goal has been identified. If you do AAT as a volunteer, you will work with a professional who will assist you in selecting goals for individual clients. In AAT, there is record keeping and you might be asked to keep some data on your progress with clients. The main characteristics of AAT are that it is done with input from a trained professional (such as a physical therapist or special-education teacher), goals and objectives for the client are identified before you begin and there is data collection or record keeping related to client progress.

Animal-assisted activities (AAA) are intended to enhance quality of life. These activities can be performed by volunteers and are basically "meet and greet" activities. Animal-assisted activities are what have been referred to in the past as "pet visitation." Animals visit patients, and there may be happy times and smiles but regular records of progress might not be kept and volunteers often make up the activities without the direction of facility staff.

An example of animal-assisted therapy is when a volunteer works with a physical therapist to teach a young child to walk. The goal is that the child will walk twenty feet without help. The volunteer's therapy dog is placed in a sit-stay and the child learns to walk to the dog. After each session, the physical therapist or volunteer records on a chart the distance the child walked.

An example of animal-assisted activity would be that the volunteer comes to a facility with a therapy cat. The volunteer and cat visit all of the clients in a day room. They tell stories and laugh and the volunteer signs out and leaves after an hour. No professional was involved in the visit, there were no goals identified for any of the clients and there was no written record of progress.

No matter what terminology is used in the setting in which you decide to volunteer, remember that when screening is completed and you begin volunteering, your animal will become more than just a pet. You and your animal will be co-therapists who work and learn together.

CHAPTER 2

Getting Started

You've heard about the field of animal-assisted therapy and you have a pet you think will be great at it. So where do you begin? The first thing you need to do is have your pet screened to ensure that it is suitable for therapy work. Then, you should get certified with a reputable therapy group. Screening and certification are procedures that will make you and your pet more credible to a facility. The screening process is a way to have some unbiased observers tell you if your animal has a suitable temperament and appropriate behavior for therapy work. The certification process that follows screening will result in your having liability insurance for your pet through an organized therapy group.

THE IMPORTANCE OF SCREENING

Potential therapy animals should complete a comprehensive screening in three major areas: health, behavior/training and temperament.

Health screening, done by a veterinarian, determines if an animal is healthy and free from disease. This protects both the clients in a facility and your animal. As a responsible person, you would not want to put clients at risk by exposing them to an animal that

Health screening ensures that therapy animals are healthy.

is not healthy. Also, you would not want your pet to be working in a therapy setting if it had a health problem that could be worsened by increased activity or stress.

Animals who work in therapy settings must also have appropriate behavior for therapy work. If you are going to a nursing home, you will not be a welcomed visitor if you bring a bird that screeches constantly. In the case of dogs and some other animals, appropriate behavior is very closely related to training. A beautiful, healthy dog is not a suitable therapy dog if it jumps on everyone it sees without an invitation.

Finally, an animal may pass the veterinary screening and be very well trained, but may not be a good candidate for therapy work due to temperament. Some animals, while they may behave wonderfully and be very loving toward their owners, just aren't ideal for doing therapy work. These animals may become stressed in unfamiliar settings or around clients who may have unpredictable behavior. Other animals may care for their owners so

Suitable therapy animals are interested in people other than their owners.

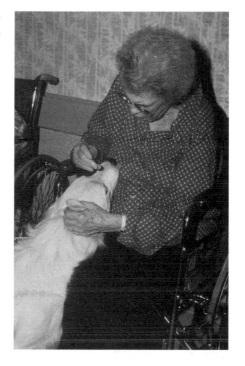

much, that they aren't at all interested in interacting with a new person. These animals would not make a client feel loved or cared for. For these reasons, screening animals for therapy work is extremely important.

THE IMPORTANCE OF LIABILITY INSURANCE

Pet owners who are willing to volunteer their time to share their pets with others are generally caring people who do everything possible to make sure that nothing goes wrong on a therapy visit. Unfortunately, accidents do happen. It is simply not responsible to volunteer with your pet unless you are covered by liability insurance! Liability insurance is insurance that will cover costs in the event that you or your animal harm someone or cause an accident while volunteering.

There are two types of liability insurance: primary and secondary. If you have primary liability insurance coverage, the insurance pays any necessary costs or charges as soon as you file the claim. If you have secondary insurance coverage, the insurance is considered a back-up to other policies that you may have, such as your homeowner's insurance.

Many volunteers are unaware of the types of claims that would be covered on their homeowner's insurance policies in the event of an incident on a therapy visit. If you are going to volunteer with your pet, you should find out what kind of coverage your homeowner's and other personal insurance policies provide. You should also understand the coverage that is provided by the therapy group that you choose to join, and whether the group's insurance provides primary or secondary coverage.

ORGANIZED THERAPY GROUPS

In order to get your animal screened and certified for therapy work, you can contact an organized therapy organization and you will be directed to evaluators in your area. There are several large, national organizations that certify animals and handlers for therapy work. The largest, most well-known therapy groups at this time include Delta Society and the Delta Society Pet Partners Program, St. John Ambulance Therapy Dogs in Canada, Therapy Dogs Inc. and Therapy Dogs International.

The standards and screening requirements for these groups vary. Be aware that standards for national therapy groups are minimum standards only. Local programs may require that some additional standards be met prior to your first visit. For example, many hospice programs will require that volunteers complete special training related to techniques for dealing with family members of people who are dying. Many facilities for people with AIDS or communicable diseases require that volunteers receive extensive training on infection control procedures.

DELTA SOCIETY

Delta Society was founded as a non-profit organization in 1977. The mission of Delta Society is to "increase recognition of the

Delta Society offers hands-on workshops for volunteers and animal evaluators.

mutually nurturing relationship between people and animals, and to establish services by animals to aid people with health difficulties, and physical and emotional challenges."

Delta Society goals include: 1) to provide quality service programs by educating and training professionals and volunteers, 2) to advocate the benefits of responsible contact with animals and nature and 3) to generate and transfer new knowledge about interactions with animals and nature.

The early history of Delta Society goes back to informal meetings of the People Pet Partnership. These meetings were held in the basement of Leo Bustad, DVM, who is the President Emeritus of Delta Society. Bustad is a leader in the study of the human–animal bond. The building that houses the Washington State

University College of Veterinary Medicine bears his name. He was a visionary who saw a need for a group such as Delta Society. Working with Linda Hines, Terry Ryan and some other devoted people, his vision became a reality.

Delta Society is now a national organization, with offices in Renton, Washington, and New York City. Delta Society has an office staff of paid employees in Renton. The organization is largely funded by private contributions. Delta Society has a library of materials relating to animal-assisted therapy. Materials can be purchased and borrowed for a small fee. Delta Society has a Board of Directors that includes leaders of large corporations and businesses. National committees exist on topics such as Research, Therapy Dogs, and Curriculum; committee projects are completed by Delta members and volunteers.

In the past, Delta Society has had an annual conference or members have been encouraged to attend international conferences relating to the human–animal bond. In the future, there may be some changes in the ways in which Delta offers education and training to its members, and there may be an increase in regional and local conferences and workshops. The Delta Society offers regional workshops for volunteers; a curriculum for training therapy dogs has been developed by a Delta Society committee. There are workshops and certification programs for both volunteer instructors and animal evaluators.

Delta Society gives annual awards in several categories to honor exceptional human–animal teams. Categories vary from year to year, but past honorees have included Therapy Animal of the Year, Therapy Dog of the Year, Service Dog of the Year and Service to an Institution Award.

For people who are committed to animal-assisted therapy and want to make a financial contribution, Delta Society has a "Caring Community" whereby individuals can name Delta Society as a beneficiary in their wills through living trusts.

Delta Society has a general membership fee of $35. This entitles the donor to regular mailings from Delta as well as a subscription to *Interactions*, a magazine that includes feature stories and updates on animal-assisted therapy. *Anthrozoos*, a scientific, research-oriented journal, is available for an additional sub-scription fee.

Delta Society members include academics, researchers, veteri-narians, teachers, nurses, doctors, administrators, psychologists, social workers, dog trainers and people who simply want to vol-unteer with their pets. Because so many of the members were interested in volunteering with their pets, in 1990 Delta Society formed a special program called "Pet Partners."

DELTA'S PET PARTNERS PROGRAM

The Pet Partners Program registers animal–human teams that successfully complete health and temperament screening and vol-unteer training. Through Pet Partners, dogs, cats, horses, birds, rabbits and other animals can be registered as therapy animals. Exotic or wild animals or birds of prey cannot be registered as Pet Partners.

Pet Partners teams visit nursing homes, hospitals, schools, pris-ons, hospices and other types of patient facilities. Pet Partners is considered a service program and members who volunteer with their pets include pet owners, therapists, educators, health profes-sionals and veterinarians.

Individuals whose animals do not pass screening are welcome to register as Pet Partners without an animal. Volunteers without animals can go on therapy visits with other volunteers and their pets, or they can do work that does not involve visiting, such as staffing a booth at a county fair or giving a talk at a community group's meeting.

Pet Partners receive an identification card that must be renewed every two years. If Pet Partners work with an animal, the animal and volunteer's picture is on the ID card. Animals are recertified every two years by submitting current veterinary information and a statement signed by a health care professional indicating that the volunteer and animal have participated suc-cessfully in therapy visits over the past two years.

The Pet Partners Program requires that not only the animal part of the therapy team be competent, but that the human at the other end of the leash is competent as well. Pet Partners volunteers must receive a minimum level of instruction on how to participate in a therapy visit. If there are enough interested volunteers to cover the costs, a Delta Society Pet Partners instructor can come to your area to provide training in a one- or two-day workshop. If this is not possible, as a volunteer, you can receive the necessary training through the Pet Partners Home Study course available from the Delta Society. In addition to the training, you will need to submit a form showing that you have volunteered in a facility similar to the one you and your animal will be visiting.

Benefits of the Pet Partners Program

Pet Partners qualify for personal liability insurance. In the case of Pet Partners, insurance is considered secondary insurance. In addition to receiving insurance, Pet Partners receive the Pet Partners newsletter six times per year. The Pet Partners newsletter contains practical tips and "how-to" information for volunteers.

In 1995, the registration fee for Pet Partners was $35. This fee is separate from the regular Delta Society membership fee. In 1994, Nakako Yamamoto and her dog, Henry, were honored at a special ceremony at the Jewish Home and Hospital for the Aged in New York City. Yamamoto and Henry were the 1,000th registered Pet Partners team. By 1995, there were 1,500 registered Pet Partners, and it was expected that the number of registered Pet Partners teams would double in 1996.

Screening Your Animal for Pet Partners

The Pet Partners Program requires that the animal complete a three-part screening: a veterinary screening, the Pet Partners Aptitude Test (which is equivalent to a temperament test) and the Pet Partners Skills Test (which is a test of behavior/training).

The **veterinary screening** for the Pet Partners Program requires that each animal receive a complete medical check-up. In the physical examination, veterinarians complete a detailed check of all areas of the animal's body including the eyes, ears, nose, throat, mouth, head and neck, withers and back, thorax, heart, abdomen, mammary glands and genitalia, legs and feet, locomotion, skin, anus and rectum and general appearance. The veterinarian lists any medical problems that may affect the animal's ability to perform therapy work. In addition to the complete medical examination, the veterinary screening includes information on the animal's vaccines and medical tests.

For dogs, vaccines and tests reviewed include a parasite control program and current updated vaccines such as DHLPP and rabies. Other things a veterinarian may check for include Bordatella, Corona, Lyme disease and heartworm disease/prevention.

For cats, the veterinarian will check tests and vaccines such as FVRCP, FeLV, rabies and FIV.

Horses, as with all other animals screened for Pet Partners, receive a complete physical examination, and appropriate immunizations or vaccines are checked. Depending on geography and other factors, these may include flu, tetanus, rhino, WEE/EEE and VEE.

Vaccines and medical tests for farm animals that are appropriate for each species are completed including clostridium, tetanus, brucellosis, erysipelas, pasturella and scraping for skin mites.

In the veterinary screening for birds, veterinarians will complete a Chlamydial screen and check for Psittacosis. Rabbits, guinea pigs and other small animals may have Chlamydial and salmonella screening during the veterinary check.

The **Pet Partners Aptitude Test** (PPAT) is the Pet Partners version of a temperament test.

In the past, temperament tests used by dog trainers involved temperament evaluators jumping out from behind walls and opening umbrellas to see if an animal reacted in an acceptable manner to unexpected stimuli. The thinking was that if the dog didn't shred the umbrella or the evaluator, the behavior would generalize to other settings and when this dog encountered a person coming quickly around a corner in a wheelchair, it would react acceptably. The whole field of temperament testing is changing and moving toward tests that are more practical and functional.

The Pet Partners Aptitude Test was developed after extensive research in the field. Over 600 therapy dog evaluators were interviewed for examples of therapy settings that therapy animals should be able to handle. The PPAT is a simulated therapy visit, ranging from a quiet "client" petting the dog to a group of more active "clients" crowding around to visit the dog. In the PPAT, the clients are actually volunteers posing as clients.

The Pet Partners test was called an "aptitude" test rather than a temperament test because the notions that some people have about "temperament" can be misleading. Many people believe that temperament is permanent and dogs are born with a good temperament or bad temperament. In years of working with therapy dogs, Delta Society animal evaluators saw a number of dogs fail items on a temperament test. Later, with training and socialization, those same dogs passed the test with no trouble and went on to become good therapy dogs.

One example is a Sheltie whose owner was eager to get involved in therapy work. She loved her dog and the dog was very well behaved at home. When the dog went to be evaluated as a therapy dog, she was nervous around unfamiliar evaluators and health-care equipment such as wheelchairs. Because she did not appear to be enjoying the simulated therapy work, she failed the test.

It turned out that this dog did not have a bad temperament. She simply had not been adequately socialized. The owner was instructed to expose her to more people and different situations. She spent time exposing the dog to new people and health-care equipment. In a matter of weeks, the dog passed the test not even looking like the same animal that had been tested weeks before. Because of situations like this one, the PPAT uses the word "aptitude" rather than temperament to indicate that the skills are behaviors that dogs have the potential or aptitude to learn.

The Pet Partners Aptitude Test has ten items that are scored as Pass, Fail or Needs Work. The "needs work" category gives animals with problems a chance to work on skills and try the test again at a later time.

1. *Overall Exam.* This test shows that the animal will accept and be comfortable when it is examined by a

Evaluations of potential therapy animals should include functional behaviors such as accepting hugs.

stranger. The evaluator will observe your animal and examine each part of the body.

The evaluator will manipulate sensitive areas of the animal—such as the flanks, abdomen and mouth—to ensure that if a client (a young child for example) touched the animal on the mouth or flank the animal would not respond by biting. Evaluators are certified, and as a part of their training, it is made clear that animals are never to be handled in a manner that is rough and inhumane.

2. ***Exuberant and clumsy petting.*** This test shows that the animal will maintain self-control if someone tries to pet it in a clumsy fashion. This test simulates clients who may not have good motor control and who pet the animal with clumsy movements. The evaluator will pet your animal in a clumsy manner. The evaluator might use an excited, high-pitched voice or clap. Smaller, more fragile animals should be handled more gently by the evaluator.

3. ***Restraining hug.*** The main purpose of this test item is to show that the animal will accept a restraining hug.

The evaluator will lean over and hug large and medium-sized dogs around the shoulders. Smaller dogs and other animals might be picked up and held against the evaluator's cheek or chest. In so many settings, clients will want to hug your therapy animal, and it is important to know if animals will accept hugs.

4. **Staggering/gesturing individual.** The purpose of this test is to show that your animal feels comfortable and does not become overly stressed when a person acting in an unusual manner approaches. The evaluator will move toward your animal staggering and weaving. The evaluator might be wearing a shawl or using a cane. As evaluators approach animals during this test, they might yell or wave their arms.

5. **Angry yelling.** The purpose of this test is to demonstrate that the animal will not be upset or overly stressed in an environment where there may be people yelling. Evaluators will approach your animal and yell. Your animal may startle, but should recover quickly.

6. **Bumped from behind.** The purpose of this test is to show that the animal can recover if accidentally bumped by a person. This test is for larger dogs; for small dogs and other animals, the evaluator will simply make a noise behind the animal.

7. **Crowded petting.** The purpose of this test is to show that the dog will permit petting by several people at once. At least three evaluators will crowd around the animal and begin to pet it. One of the evaluators will be using health-care equipment.

8. **Held by a stranger.** The purpose of this test is to show that the animal can be left for a brief period of time with a stranger. The evaluator will say something to you like, "Would you like us to watch your pet while you make your phone call?" With you out of sight, the evaluator will hold the leash of your dog for three minutes. If your animal is a cat, bird or other animal, the evaluator will hold the animal in the animal's carrying cage or basket.

This test is practical in therapy settings because there are times when you will need to make a call or go to the restroom.

9. ***Overall sociability.*** The purpose of this test is for the evaluator to score the animal for overall interest in people. In this test, the evaluator will observe your animal to see if it is happy and comfortable in the presence of other people.

10. ***Overall reaction.*** The purpose of this test is to show how well you and your pet work together as a team in settings that may be unpredictable. The evaluator will watch to see if you have good control of the animal and if the animal would be reliable in a therapy setting.

Keep in mind that this test should be done in a humane manner. Evaluators should not hurt your animal in any way by pinching it or pulling hair. However, it is necessary to assess the animal's reaction to some things that routinely happen in therapy settings.

If you feel that you would not like to have your animal exposed to yelling or being accidentally bumped, you may want to reconsider volunteering with your animal in a therapy setting. Most therapy settings serve clients with special needs. The direct observations in therapy settings indicate that the behaviors tested on the PPAT are likely to occur in many therapy settings with special needs clients.

The **Pet Partners Skills Test** is the portion of the Pet Partners screening that tests to ensure animals have adequate training and appropriate behavior for therapy settings. The Pet Partners Skills Test is actually the American Kennel Club's (AKC) Canine Good Citizen Test (CGC) with some minor modifications. Delta Society was granted permission from the American Kennel Club to use the CGC provided that appropriate credits are given in written materials.

The modifications that were made to the Canine Good Citizen Test in order to make it the Pet Partners Skills Test are: 1) Pet Partners requires that health-care equipment be used in the test;

Many therapy organizations use the AKC's Canine Good Citizen Test as part of screening.
Courtesy of Betty and Charlie O'Hara

this is not a requirement for the AKC version of the CGC. 2) Pet Partners needed to change the name of the Canine Good Citizen Test for screening purposes because they use the test for screening other animals.

If dogs go through the Pet Partners version of the test and do not complete all ten items, they may not receive the AKC's Canine Good Citizen certificate.

THE AKC CANINE GOOD CITIZEN TEST

The American Kennel Club's Canine Good Citizen Test (CGC) was introduced in 1988. The program is based on the premise that all dogs should have sufficient training to be under control at all times both at home and in the community. The CGC tests good manners, not temperament, so most of the test involves learned behaviors. Since the Canine Good Citizen Test was introduced, it has been adopted as a screening tool for several therapy dog organizations. In addition to the United States, the test has been implemented in Canada, England, Australia, and Japan. Japanese supporters of the CGC have worked hard to have the test adopted into the culture. Japanese owners of dogs who are CGC certified carry a wallet card that can be used to gain admission to hotels and other public buildings. In the United States, some cities have CGC-certified neighborhoods, and there is CGC legislation in several states.

As mentioned previously, the CGC test has ten parts, or individual tests. The test has been modified once since it began. Currently, the **ten CGC tests** are:

1. *Accepting a friendly stranger.* This test demonstrates that the dog will allow a friendly stranger to approach it and speak to the handler in a natural everyday situation. The evaluator will shake hands and exchange pleasantries. The dog must show no sign of resentment or shyness and must not break position or try to go to the evaluator.

2. *Sitting politely for petting.* This test demonstrates that the dog will allow a friendly stranger to touch it while it is with its handler. The evaluator pets the dog and then circles the dog and handler. The dog must show no signs of shyness or resentment.

3. *Appearance and grooming.* This test shows that the dog will welcome being groomed and examined and will permit a stranger to do so. It also demonstrates the owner's care, concern and responsibility. The evaluator inspects the dog, then combs or brushes the dog and lightly examines the ears and each front paw.

4. *Out for a walk (Walking on loose leash).* This test shows that the handler is in control of the dog. The evaluator may use a pre-plotted course or may direct the handler/dog team by issuing instructions or commands. There must be a left turn, a right turn and an about turn, with at least one stop in between and another at the end. The dog need not be perfectly aligned with the handler and need not sit when the handler stops.

5. ***Walking through a crowd.*** This test shows that the dog can move about politely in pedestrian traffic and is under control in public places. The dog and handler walk around and pass close to several people. The dog may show some interest in the strangers, without appearing over exuberant, shy or resentful.

6. ***Sit and down on command/staying in place.*** This test shows that the dog has training, will respond to the handler's command to sit and down and will remain in the place commanded by the handler (sit or down position, whichever the handler prefers). The handler may take a reasonable amount of time and use more than one command.

7. ***Coming when called.*** This test demonstrates the dog will come when called. The handler will walk ten feet from the dog, turn to face the dog and will call the dog. The handler may use body language and encouragement when calling the dog. The dog is on the twenty-foot line used in the previous exercise for this test.

8. ***Reaction to another dog.*** This test shows that the dog can behave politely around other dogs. Two handlers and their dogs approach each other from a distance of about ten yards, stop, shake hands and exchange pleasantries and continue on for about five yards. The dogs should show no more than a casual interest in each other.

9. ***Reactions to distractions.*** This test shows that the dog is confident at all times when faced with common distracting situations. The dog may express a natural interest and curiosity and may appear slightly startled, but should not panic, try to run away, show aggressiveness or bark.

10. ***Supervised separation.*** This test shows that a dog can be left with a person other than the owner, if necessary, and will maintain its training and good manners. Evaluators will say something like, "Would you like me to watch your dog while you make your call?" to add a touch of reality. The dog will be attached to a six-foot line held by

an evaluator and does not have to stay in position but should not continually bark, whine, howl, pace unnecessarily or show anything other than mild agitation or nervousness.

JOINING DELTA SOCIETY'S PET PARTNERS

In summary, to become certified as a Pet Partner, your animal must pass 1) veterinary screening, 2) aptitude testing (temperament) and 3) a skills test (behaviors). In addition, as the human component of the team, you will be required to complete volunteer training and some volunteer hours in a facility prior to joining Pet Partners. Delta Society has a Code of Ethics for people who work in animal-assisted therapy settings.

The **Delta Society Code of Ethics** states that animal-assisted therapy and activities personnel will 1) treat people, animals and nature with respect, dignity and sensitivity; 2) promote quality of life in their work; 3) abide by the professional ethics of their respective professions and/or organizations; 4) perform duties commensurate with their training and position; and 5) comply with all applicable Delta Society policies, and local, state and federal laws relating to their work.

For more information on the Pet Partners Program or Delta Society, contact: Delta Society, 289 Perimeter Road East, Renton, WA 98055-1329, (206)226-7357.

ST. JOHN AMBULANCE THERAPY DOGS

Based in Canada, St. John Ambulance describes itself as the oldest charity in the world. It's 999 years old. St. John Ambulance has served communities of Canada for nearly 1,000 years in the areas of first aid, ambulance service and general care.

In June 1992, the St. John Ambulance Therapy Dog Program was started in Peterborough. The program began with six dogs and eight people as an extension to regular care provided by the organization. Founders of the therapy dog program were seeing many lonely, elderly, sick people in nursing homes and hospitals who no longer experienced the joys of everyday living.

When it became clear that the therapy dogs were making a valuable contribution, volunteers were recruited from local areas. In the early days, the program operated as a chapter of Therapy Dogs International (TDI). The group left TDI in order to facilitate expansion and to develop their own standards. Volunteers visit a specified case load of clients so that clients can get to know them and develop a bond.

As of 1995, St. John Ambulance Therapy Dogs had over 1,500 dogs making regular visits in Ontario. The program is being expanded into Alberta. Over 24,000 clients receive services from the St. John program and the volunteers provide 2,200 hours per week of documented service.

All the dogs have been tested by one of the group's Certified Evaluators. Dogs and handlers are insured for two million dollars through third party insurance. Handlers are supplied with uniforms that consist of a tag for the dog, and a golf shirt or sweatshirt with the St. John logo for the owner. Benefits such as shirts and tags are provided at no cost once dogs qualify for therapy work. Volunteers visit nursing homes, hospitals, day centers and schools for children with special needs. They also take part in many community activities such as parades and fairs.

St. John Therapy Dogs have adopted the American Kennel Club's Canine Good Citizen Test (CGC) as a basic screening tool. The CGC is considered an introductory test. If the dog passes the CGC and is thought to be appropriate for therapy work, a more advanced test (Level 1) is administered. The Level 1 test simulates scenarios that one would find in a nursing home or hospital setting. Level 2 in this program is the first ten weeks of actual visiting. Four of the visits are accompanied by either an evaluator or an experienced coordinator. After the first four visits are completed successfully, the volunteer visits an additional six weeks independently. If all of those steps are completed satisfactorily, a therapy dog certificate is issued.

As of 1995, the forty certified evaluators of St. John Therapy Dogs have tested over 3,500 dogs using the CGC test. About 15 percent of the dogs fail the CGC and do not participate in therapy work.

Evaluators for St. John Therapy Dogs include obedience judges, veterinarians and obedience teachers with at least six years experience in working with and handling dogs. Evaluators are reassessed each year, and if individuals do not quite have the qualifications to be an evaluator, they can apply to be an assistant evaluator. Evaluators must complete a seminar, provide proof of hands-on experience with dogs and provide references as to their knowledge of dog breeds and general dog behavior.

The job of evaluators is to offer the CGC on behalf of St. John Ambulance Therapy Dogs in order to assess both the canine and handler for temperament, cleanliness, sociability and confidence. Neither should exhibit apprehension or excessive nervousness in any of the categories.

Evaluators are required to be at least auxiliary members with St. John Ambulance and conform to the rules of conduct of the organization. Evaluators must complete a seminar and supply proof of hands-on experience with a variety of breeds. They also should have a good understanding of basic dog behavior—both practical and theoretical.

Evaluators are expected to show an eagerness to update knowledge by attending seminars and reading appropriate materials. They are expected to hold CGC tests and turn in paperwork in a timely manner. Evaluators re-test any dog wishing to join the St. John program which has previously earned a CGC.

The St. John program has some additional requirements for evaluators including procedures for notifying the chief evaluator of CGC tests. Assistant evaluators are trained to give the CGC. An experienced panel of three people observes assistant evaluators before they achieve evaluator status.

For more information on the St. John Ambulance Therapy Dog program, contact: Doreen A. Newell, Provincial Coordinator, St. John Ambulance Therapy Dogs, 1199 Deyell 3rd Line, Millbrook, Ontario, L0A 1G0, (705)932-3626.

THERAPY DOGS INCORPORATED

Therapy Dogs Incorporated was founded by Jack and Ann Butrick. The Butricks were originally members of Therapy Dogs

Jack Butrick, founder of Therapy Dogs Incorporated.

International (see below) and they started Therapy Dogs Incorporated in 1990. People tend to get confused about the differences in these two groups, partly because they share some history and because they both have the initials TDI. Therapy Dogs Incorporated goes by the full name of the organization, or Therapy Dogs, Inc.

Jack Butrick was another pioneer in the history of animal-assisted therapy. He had a dream of creating a group of volunteers who worked with therapy dogs.

Many years ago, Butrick did most of the writing for a therapy dog newsletter. His was a "stream of consciousness" style of writing. He named and described as many volunteers as possible in a short space, which made the newsletter difficult to read. When Therapy Dogs Incorporated was formed, the newsletter format changed. The current newsletter includes plenty of photos and gives members a chance to showcase their work.

While he performed demonstrations and visits with his dog, one of Jack Butrick's greatest strengths was his ability to do therapy work. Some early videotapes show him with his Doberman Pinscher, J.R., working with a variety of populations, ranging from young children to seniors in nursing homes. In the presence of professionals such as physical therapists and special education teachers, Butrick worked on specific goals and objectives and achieved results. A young autistic boy who stood shrieking and flapping his hands would follow Butrick's commands to give instructions to a therapy dog. Normally engaged in self-stimulatory hand-flapping, the child would attend to the task of holding a leash or walking with the dog. Butrick was using animals to teach measurable goals and objectives (commonplace now) when most people were excited about simply visiting with the animals.

In laying the groundwork for Therapy Dogs Incorporated, Jack and Ann Butrick stressed the importance of a well-trained dog as a therapy partner. When you have a dog who can follow your instructions, the gains that can be made in animal-assisted therapy are significant. In addition to formal obedience training, many members have followed Butrick's model and taught their dogs a number of tricks. Therapy Dogs Incorporated members have discovered that in therapy settings, tricks are crowd pleasers and conversation starters.

Jack Butrick died on July 25, 1992. He had a heart attack immediately after performing in a parade with one of his therapy dogs. Ann Butrick has assumed the administrative responsibilities of Therapy Dogs Incorporated and the membership has seen a steady increase over the years.

CHANGING TEARS INTO SMILES

The goal of Therapy Dogs Incorporated is to help owners of both obedience and conformation, purebred and mixed breed dogs use dogs for therapy work in various places such as nursing homes, hospitals and schools, as well as work with people who have mental and physical handicaps. An objective of Therapy Dogs Incorporated is to form a network of people who are willing to share their animals with others. The motto of Therapy Dogs Incorporated is, "Change Tears into Smiles—Help the Forgotten to Laugh."

Therapy Dogs Incorporated has guidelines for volunteers and a member handbook. The organization has a board of directors, and by-laws and financial statements are provided to the membership annually. Members receive photo ID cards and they can purchase patches, pins and other items bearing the group's logo. Therapy Dogs Incorporated provides primary liability insurance coverage for dogs and handlers.

The application for registration may give the impression that in order to register with Therapy Dogs Incorporated, one simply needs to fill out the form and send in a check. This is not the case; there is a preliminary test that must be taken prior to any visit with Therapy Dogs Incorporated. Then, before being certified, each person must be observed three times in a therapy setting by an approved observer. Therapy Dogs Incorporated maintains a list of approved tester/observers.

In 1995, the cost of joining Therapy Dogs Incorporated was $15 for an individual membership and $20 for a family membership. The fee for 4-H handlers was $5, and the fee for additional dogs was $2 per dog.

For more information on Therapy Dogs Incorporated, contact: Therapy Dogs, Inc., 2416 East Fox Farm Rd., Cheyenne, WY 82007, (307) 638-3223.

THERAPY DOGS INTERNATIONAL (TDI)

As with other major therapy groups, Therapy Dogs International (TDI) came about as the result of one person who recognized the therapeutic benefits of pets. In the case of TDI, the pioneer was Elaine Smith.

Elaine Smith was a registered nurse in England when she recognized the value of pets for people who were confined. "The therapeutic value of pets has been acknowledged in England for more

Elaine Smith, TDI, at the signing of a therapy dog bill in 1984.

than thirty years," Smith said in an interview several years ago. Smith worked with dogs in therapy settings and had good results. Using her German Shepherd, Phila, and her Shetland Sheepdog, Genny, in therapy sessions, Smith got a woman to talk who hadn't spoken in years. When she came to the United States, Smith brought the concept of therapy dogs with her. She began TDI in 1976, making it the oldest organization for therapy dogs in this country.

As early as 1982, Smith was working with Senator Louis Bassano to define terms related to therapy and service animals. She was instrumental in drafting legislation to allow elderly people in residential facilities to have pets.

When Smith worked on defining the terms related to service animals and therapy dogs, the field of actual service dogs (e.g., guide dogs, hearing dogs) was young and many of the current standards had not yet been developed. The original yellow tag for therapy dogs from TDI said, "I am a service dog."

Current definitions of therapy and service animals make a clear distinction between the two, and the term service dog is no longer legally correct or appropriate for dogs who perform animal-assisted therapy work. TDI tags now indicate that the dogs are therapy dogs.

TDI dogs are tested by TDI-certified evaluators. The American Kennel Club's Canine Good Citizen Test is used as an evaluation tool. In addition, a form is completed that provides information regarding the dog's behavior.

In order to become a certified evaluator, a form is completed and there is an additional fee. TDI has an evaluator coordinator who is available to answer evaluator questions.

TDI provides members with secondary liability insurance. Members can purchase T-shirts, patches, and other products with the TDI logo. TDI produces a newsletter that is distributed to members. In 1995, TDI had approximately 5,000 members and had registered more than 10,000 dogs. Much of TDI's office work is done by volunteers. The organization does have an office and a paid staff person was hired in 1995.

The cost to join TDI is $20 with a $5 increase for each additional dog. Members are renewed every two years. For more information on TDI, contact: Therapy Dogs International, 6 Hilltop Rd., Mendham, NJ 07945, (201)543-0888.

OTHER GROUPS

There are some groups whose primary purpose is to promote the cause of animal-assisted therapy but do not register volunteers and their pets. One such group is Alpha Affiliates, Inc.

Alpha Affiliates, Inc., was founded in 1987. It is an all-volunteer, non-profit organization that focuses on education and scientific inquiry involving human–animal interactions.

Alpha Affiliates, Inc., supports studies about the human–animal bond, organizes educational seminars, animal-assisted therapy workshops and humane education sessions. The group publishes a newsletter called *Alpha Bits*, which provides current information on topics related to the human–animal bond. *Alpha Bits* is described as "Your link between people and the benefits of animals." *Alpha Bits* is a very professional publication, full of the latest information on the human–animal bond. A newsletter subscription is $10.

For more information on Alpha Affiliates, Inc., contact: Alpha Affiliates, Inc., 103 Washington St., Suite 362, Morristown, NJ 07960, (201) 539-2770.

THE BENEFITS OF JOINING AN ORGANIZED GROUP

In addition to having liability insurance, one of the most significant benefits of joining an organized, recognized animal-assisted therapy group is that, as a volunteer, you will become a part of a network that is like a family. You'll be able to have contact with other well-trained volunteers and their pets, and if you ever have a problem, you won't feel that you have to address it on your own. When you are trying to do a good job and make a contribution with your pet, you shouldn't have to struggle to figure out how to best work with a person with a certain type of disability or problem. As part of an established network, you will have colleagues and friends that you can learn from.

In addition to belonging to a national animal-assisted therapy group, you may have a local group of people and pets in your area that are interested in therapy work. Membership in a local group can be fun, and it is nice to be able to go on visits with others with whom you share common experiences, such as volunteering at the same facilities.

Membership in a nationally recognized group will give you credibility with facilities. There are some well-known dog trainers who take pride in approaching facilities and giving demonstrations of animal-assisted therapy. When asked if their dogs are certified, they respond as though such a practice is beneath them. There is too much at stake in this field for any of us to be out there swimming around on our own. While we may have differences in opinions about the groups we choose to join, we should all adhere to some formal standards. If one person can go to a facility with no training or certification, then everyone can. A major incident could result in all of us losing access to facilities.

Learning a Lesson

These concerns are based on reality. I discovered the reality of the problems uncertified volunteers and pets can cause in my own backyard.

I was a behavioral consultant to the local school district. Many of the teachers I knew were aware that I had certified therapy dogs. Over a period of several years, I got invitations to go into classrooms with my dogs. Everything seemed fine. Teachers invited me to come to classes, I went, and children benefited from interactions with the therapy dogs. After I had done this for several years, I got involved in finding placements for ten newly certified volunteers who wanted to work with children. Because I knew people in the school system, I was elected to call an administrator about placing these new volunteers.

"I'm calling out of the context of my job," I started. "There is a field called animal-assisted therapy where. . ." I was interrupted by the administrator.

"I know all about it," she said. "It's where they take dogs to nursing homes."

"Well, yes, nursing homes and schools and other facilities. These volunteers would like to work in the schools," I continued.

"Not in our schools," she informed me. "We have a school board policy preventing any dogs on our campuses with the exception of police and sheriffs' dogs involved in drug awareness education."

Imagine my surprise. Not only had I been busy visiting classrooms, but I was making a practice of telling everyone in the country about it. I knew about people from several groups taking their dogs to the schools. I had been invited by teachers from schools all over the district to bring my dogs to their classes. It never dawned on me that teachers would invite me to do something that was in violation of a district policy. I started asking about the history of the policy. Sure enough, some volunteers were taking dogs that were not certified or well-trained to a particular school.

While the teachers in the classes they were visiting seemed satisfied, parents and other staff observing the behavior of the dogs were concerned enough to make calls to the school board. The volunteers had no liability insurance. They were not a part of a national program and were uneducated about animal-assisted therapy. They were not well-enough informed to give a convincing presentation of the benefits of having animals visit classrooms. They were unable to say that the dogs had been tested for behavior and temperament by certified evaluators. They had no national group they could call for assistance. Their behavior resulted in a policy of "no animals in schools" for everyone.

CHOOSING THE THERAPY GROUP FOR YOU

People are different. Some of us like a lot of structure and direction while others feel too regulated by a lot of structure and want to be more independent. Animal-assisted therapy groups have differences and provide a different range of services. When deciding on the animal-assisted therapy group that is best for you, make an educated, informed choice. Look at the materials the group produces. Call and talk to someone about the group. Watch some of the volunteers from the group in action. Think about the level of service and involvement you want from a therapy organization.

After you join and have been a member for a while, decide if you are satisfied with how you are treated as a member. Can you call someone and have your questions answered? Do you get materials such as newsletters in a regular, timely manner? Do you ever hear from the group other than when it is time to send money?

Most therapy groups are non-profit organizations. This means that as a member, you should see an annual financial report and the group should have independent audits. There should be annual meetings of the board of directors and the members, and you should be aware and given an opportunity to express your needs as a member at these meetings.

As animal-assisted therapy becomes better recognized, there will probably be an increase in the number of therapy groups that exist. Making sure that you are a smart consumer will help you and your pet have a positive experience in the group that you have decided to join.

GETTING STARTED AT A FACILITY

You've contacted all the major therapy organizations. You've reviewed a ton of materials from all of them and you've talked to some of their members. "What is so great about this group?" and "Why should I join this group instead of another?" are the kinds of questions you've asked.

You've made your choice. You've taken your animal to the screening and you've been certified. Congratulations! You're ready to start volunteering at a facility. You either join a local group that will place you in a facility or you make phone calls and visits and obtain your own placement. As you begin volunteering, there are some things to watch out for.

MY FIRST VISIT

When I started volunteering, I called a local therapy program after seeing an ad in the paper. I was soon assigned to a nursing home and given the name of the activity director who was to be my contact person.

I made the first visit by myself. When I arrived, the activity director had prepared a list of clients who would be on my case-load. I was told that the visits were to last one hour. She gave me a list of twenty client names and a "data sheet." The data sheet was being used at all of the facilities that were under contract with a local therapy program. On the first visit I was supposed to intro-duce myself and my dog to the clients. After that visit, I was instructed to locate each person, ask the questions on the data sheet, record the answers, and move on to the next person.

Guided by the information on the data sheet, I was to enter a room and start asking questions. "Hi, do you remember my name?" Score yes or no. "Do you remember my dog's name?" Score yes or no. "What is your name?" Score correct or incorrect. "What day is it?" Score correct or incorrect. "Do you know what time it is?" Score correct or incorrect. After recording the responses to those five questions, I was to tell the client when I'd be back for the next visit as I left to find the next person.

I did this for one client and then went straight to the activity director's office to tell her I was on my way to the local program office to help them change their procedures. How in the world did they come up with this? Apparently one of the volunteer coordinators had seen a similar checklist in a geriatrics journal and concluded this must be the thing to do with older people. What she didn't understand was that the checklist was a geriatric mental status exam. Such checklists are used to determine if a person is disoriented. A medical professional or therapist might ask those kinds of questions periodically. It is never appropriate to use those checklists as the curriculum and as an ongoing treatment plan.

It didn't take a person with graduate training to figure out the protocol for the visits was awful. Any person who had some empathy could have figured this out by asking him or herself the right question. *As you volunteer with your pet, there is one question you should constantly ask as a guide for determining if a particular practice is right in terms of both ethics and common sense. The question is, "Would I like to be treated like this?"*

Believe it or not, there was something worse happening than the data sheets when I began my first animal-assisted therapy visits. After I abandoned the question-asking, I went to find the other nineteen people on the list. The first few people enjoyed the dog and liked visiting with me. Then I came to Mrs. Wilson's room. Mrs. Wilson had Alzheimer's disease and it was in the advanced stages. She was confused and disoriented. To make it worse, she had fallen and broken her hip. She was physically restrained and confined to bed and her most common response to anything was to scream. Loud, high-pitched screaming. As I approached the bed, she screamed louder. No words, just, "AAHHH, AAAHHH," over and over, loud enough to hurt the ears of anyone within six feet of her bed.

Two things were wrong with this picture. First, the facility had no knowledge of my background in working in therapeutic settings. For all they knew, I was a volunteer who worked as a waitress. I should have never been sent to find Mrs. Wilson by myself, and a volunteer should not have been assigned a client whose behavior was so out of control.

Second, it was not at all clear that Mrs. Wilson would in any way benefit from our visit. Some of her screaming seemed to be related to pain. Before she could benefit from animal-assisted therapy, she needed medical intervention to manage the pain. Animal-assisted therapy is used with people who are in pain, but not when the pain is so bad the person is screaming.

I felt so sorry for Mrs. Wilson, I asked a nurse to check on her and went on to the next client. After visiting a few clients who liked my dog, I met Luella. She had silver braids wrapped all around her head. Her room didn't look like a nursing home room. She had her own antique furniture and she managed to somehow get past the "no rugs" rule. She had a giant rug on the floor that she'd latch-hooked herself. The dressers and tables were covered with lacy doilies. Every inch of the walls in her room were covered with some kind of country craft. She had enough picture frames covered in quilted material and eyelet lace to stock all the craft stores in the United States. I introduced myself in the doorway and told her I had been given her name as a person I should visit with the dog. "You aren't bringing that dog in my room; get that dog out of here," she demanded. "I'm sorry," I said, "I was told to visit you, I didn't realize you didn't like dogs. Maybe if I ever come without the dog, we can visit."

Luella was from the country. She had farm dogs when she was a girl and they all lived outside. "Where they belong," she said emphatically. She didn't want dog hair on her rug, not even one dog hair. She wanted to sit and make her crafts and not be disturbed by a dog or a volunteer.

I believe that Luella had the right to make that choice. I told the activity director a mistake had been made when Luella's name was added to the animal-assisted therapy list. She insisted that Luella should receive services on the grounds that, with enough exposure, she would learn to like dogs. Wrong again.

Assessing Your Environment

As you volunteer in therapy settings, you may come across procedures that have been put into place for reasons that aren't obvious at first. I was instructed to see twenty clients in one hour. Adding in the time it took me to find each client and walk down the hall, each visit was less than two minutes—hardly a quality inter-action. I was also told to continue seeing clients on the list even if they wouldn't allow me to come through the doorway of their room. "Just write that each time on the data sheet," were my instructions.

I learned this was being done to satisfy "contact hours." Some facilities have to document that they provide therapy and contact for their clients in order to be reimbursed by federal and state funding. In some cases, clients refuse to attend activities voluntar-ily and are assigned to volunteers such as visiting church people and animal-assisted therapists. That way, contact hours can be documented. If you are in a situation where the client refuses your services, it is not ethical for you to continue visiting. At such times, your national group can provide assistance by contacting the facility and talking to the appropriate people about the code of ethics for animal-assisted therapists.

ALLOWING THE CLIENTS TO CHOOSE

Clients are people. People have the right to make choices. In a set-ting like a nursing home, so much of the routine is controlled. Unless clients are independent, baths are given at a time when they can be scheduled by staff. Meals are planned by a nutrition-ist. People who no longer have their spouses and people they loved are in an environment where many of their reinforcers are gone. They no longer can choose to work in the garden that they designed themselves, or rock in the old creaky chair on their own front porch. There are a limited number of choices that can be made by clients in controlled environments.

If a client doesn't want to see your pet, don't feel rejected. The client has been given the dignity of making choices. As you begin volunteering, there will be many people who will welcome your services and whose moments you and your pet can fill with joy.

PREPARING FOR A VISIT

Each time you volunteer with any type of therapy animal, you'll want to make sure you have adequately prepared both yourself and the animal for the visit.

Handlers should be dressed and groomed in a manner that creates a professional image. Animals should always be clean when they are taken on an animal-assisted therapy visit. While a bath may not be needed every time you visit, at a minimum, animals should be brushed or combed. Ears and teeth should be clean and nails should be clipped.

EQUIPMENT TO TAKE ON A VISIT

You'll want to make sure your animal is comfortable on therapy visits and that you have the equipment needed for a successful visit. On each visit, you should take a water bowl/dish, appropriate leashes and collars, treats if appropriate, food if appropriate, a towel or sheet for presenting small animals on laps or beds, a brush or comb, crates/cages/carrying baskets, materials to clean up messes unless you have been invited to use facility supplies, necessary identification badges for you and your pet, and any data sheets, clipboards or paperwork that you might need.

PROTOCOL FOR AN ANIMAL-ASSISTED ACTIVITY VISIT

For those unfamiliar with this whole process, it can seem intimidatingly unfamiliar. So that you're prepared ahead of time, this is the typical protocol.

1. *Greeting.* Greet the client; introduce yourself and your pet if the client doesn't remember you. If clients are in a group, you can introduce yourself and your pet to the group (with something like, "Hello, everyone, my name is _____, and this is my dog, ____).

2. *Check the client's status.* In settings where there are health and medical concerns, you should briefly check the status of the client by asking, "How are you doing today?" There will be some days that clients will not wish to see you or your pet. Be cautious about reinforcing chronic complaining with no apparent health cause. Report any problems to facility staff.

3. *Choice to have pet/visitor.* Before you enter an individual client's room or begin putting a small animal into someone's lap, you should give the client choices regarding whether he or she would like to see your pet today.

4. *Choice of level of interaction.* If the client does not spontaneously begin interacting with your pet, you should give the person some choice regarding the level of interaction desired. "Would you like to pet my cat?" "Do you want me to put the guinea pig on a towel on your lap?" Before taking a client's hand to guide petting, make sure it's something the client would like to do.

5. *Content of the visit.* This can be a basic visit (involving "conversation behaviors," see below for more on these); a demonstration ("Would you like to see my dog do tricks?") or an educational visit ("Would you like to learn some things about parrots?").

6. *End of visit.* Say good-bye to the client or group. Before leaving, you should always tell clients when and if you will return.

CONVERSATION BEHAVIORS IN AN ANIMAL-ASSISTED ACTIVITIES VISIT

Like what to do when you visit, what to say can also be an awkward process for a novice volunteer. Hopefully this guideline will get you started comfortably.

1. *Give information (tell a story).* In health care settings, if you watch closely, you will be amazed at how many questions clients have to answer: "How are you feeling?" "Is your daughter coming today?" "What do you want to eat?" And so on. Too often, no one spends time simply talking with clients. This is a need you can fill by simply telling an amusing story about your pet or something you've been doing.

2. *Prompt conversation.* To encourage conversation, you can give clients some open-ended prompts such as, "That's interesting. . . tell me more."

3. *Describe the animal's or client's behavior.* "She likes it when you brush her. Did you notice how she is getting closer to you?"

4. *Get information (ask a question).* There are times when questions are appropriate—just be sure you also talk with clients without constantly questioning them. Asking a question such as, "Did you ever have a dog?" may be the key to helping you learn something about the client.

5. *Reinforce client conversation by showing your interest.* This should be genuine and sincere. When you are talking with a client who does not talk much, responses from you such as "That's interesting," or "That is so funny!" can encourage the client to talk more.

6. *Use good communication techniques.* Throughout the entire visit, you should:

   a) Smile (maybe not constantly, but you should appear to be enjoying the visit);

   b) Make sure you have good eye contact with a client;

   c) Position yourself and your animal to maximize the effectiveness of the interaction.

PART II

Which Pets Do What and Why

CHAPTER 3

Dogs

Dogs are the most commonly used pets in animal-assisted therapy. They make excellent therapists because they are not judgmental and give unconditional love to clients who may have not felt loved in a very long time. Dogs love people regardless of their appearance, problems or social status. Some of the most powerful advances in the history of animal-assisted therapy have occurred when a dog was used as a part of the treatment team.

WHICH BREED IS BEST?

There is a myth that certain breeds are better for therapy than others. A dog's breed does not matter; what does matter is the dog's behavior and characteristics as they relate to a specific setting. Dogs of any breed, pure or mixed that have passed the necessary veterinary, behavioral and temperament screening can be suitable for therapy work.

Selecting and Placing Therapy Dogs

As with all therapy animals, the important thing to remember is that there must be a balance between several variables in order to optimize therapy results. Dogs need to be matched to the client population based on client characteristics and needs. The dog's temperament and skill level also need to be considered, as do the preferences of the handler. Correct selection and placement of therapy animals involves achieving a good balance between all of these factors.

Consider the following scenario. An elderly person with a broken hip is confined to a hospital bed. The person requests a dog that can visit and stay in bed for an hour or so each day. A large dog like an Irish Wolfhound would probably not be a good choice for this particular client in this particular setting. A small dog like a Maltese or Miniature Pinscher might be a better choice as a therapy dog for this client.

On the other hand, while Miniature Pinschers would make great therapy dogs in this case, they might not be suitable at a residential facility serving hyperactive, teenage males with behavior problems.

Client Preferences

Individual clients may have preferences regarding the dogs that they would like to be visited by. One client, Mrs. Roberts, was not at all interested in visiting with my Border Collie, but every time she saw me, she asked if I could bring a Manchester Terrier. She had one named Babe more than forty years earlier. Mrs. Roberts wanted nothing to do with my dog, but every Tuesday morning she had to tell me the story of Babe.

The story was that with the prompt, "Go get daddy," Babe would go out to the shop every night at 7 p.m. to bring Mr. Roberts to dinner.

Mrs. Roberts wasn't interested in just any dog. She wanted one that reminded her of Babe, Mr. Roberts, and times long ago.

TEMPERAMENT AND TRAINING

My Border Collie had a Utility title (an advanced American Kennel Club obedience degree) and he could respond to nearly 200 commands. He was a therapy dog extraordinaire. My Welsh Springer Spaniel was a Canine Good Citizen with a Companion Dog (beginning) obedience title. People were amazed and awed when they saw the Border Collie in action. Yet, in many therapy settings, the Welsh Springer was the far better choice for a therapy dog. The Welsh was mellow. If I needed a dog that would lay on the floor and be stroked by a child who had been abused, the Welsh was perfect. The Border Collie had the training to do this and would have stayed in a down position until released, but he didn't look happy about it. For an assignment calling for a dog who liked

Therapy dogs can make holidays memorable events for clients.
Courtesy of Rocky and Natalie Sachs-Ericsson

being quiet and still, my Border Collie had the wrong temperament, even though he was trained to do it. It is important to match the dog's behavior and temperament with the therapy setting. We should all enjoy our work, including our therapy dogs.

ADVANTAGES OF USING DOGS

There are many advantages to using dogs in therapy settings. People like dogs. Dogs respond to training and can perform a wide range of tasks under instructional control; they can learn to do what you tell them to do. When you can give a dog a hand signal and have him bring a young child his shoes, you and your dog have made a friend for life. Therapy dogs wearing reindeer or bunny ears can make holidays memorable for clients by delivering gifts.

Dogs are more robust than small animals such as birds and hamsters and they are less likely to be injured by clients who have limited control of their movements. Many larger breeds of dogs can physically assist clients in tasks such as walking, unlike smaller animals like cats. Dogs are sociable. They have good eye contact and they are eager to engage in activities with another person. Fun things can be done with dogs, like playing ball. Dogs travel well to and from facilities and they do not get sick easily. Dogs increase the sociability of the handler. Dogs can receive petting and restraining hugs from clients and come out of it smiling. Plenty of people think that dogs are man's best friend.

DISADVANTAGES OF USING DOGS

Some people are allergic to dogs. Depending on the part of the country, some people believe that dogs belong outside. Dogs require a certain amount of grooming prior to visits. Depending on the breed, this grooming may be fairly extensive and time-consuming. To be good at therapy work, dogs require training. Really good therapy dogs require a lot of training. Dogs sometimes have behavior problems in therapy settings, making them difficult to handle. Some clients are afraid of dogs, and their fear may generalize to other clients. Some staff members who are afraid of dogs might attempt to sabotage the animal-assisted therapy program at a facility.

BEHAVIOR PROBLEMS IN THERAPY SETTINGS

Therapy settings are often filled with unusual smells, sounds and things to eat. Therapy dogs should have been screened and be under good behavior control before visiting. However, even the most well-behaved therapy dogs may have some minor behavior problems that will need to be corrected.

Problems related to socialization. Some dogs love people, which can be a desired trait for a therapy dog. Therapy dogs should be enthusiastic, but not over-exuberant or overly active. Dogs who jump on clients or bump into them quickly can cause injuries.

At the other extreme of socialization problems is the shy dog. Some dogs are reluctant to approach strangers. They are uncomfortable when they are not close to their handlers. These dogs

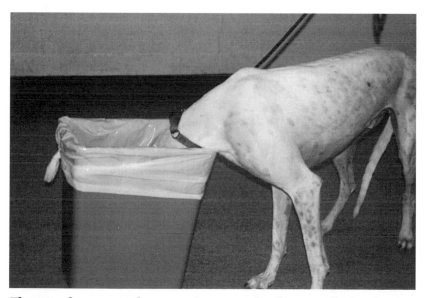

Therapy dogs must learn to ignore unfamiliar smells in therapy settings.
Courtesy of Ellen Berter and Drew

need to be better socialized, or, in some cases, they may not be appropriate for therapy work. Clients want to feel accepted and cared for by a dog. When they clap, whistle and call a dog who does not come, clients may feel rejection and failure.

Some dogs are fearful around health-care equipment. This is not so much a socialization problem as it is a problem that relates to experience and conditioning. These dogs need extra training and positive reinforcement in the presence of health-care equipment.

Inappropriate smelling. Health-care and therapy settings are full of all kinds of unusual smells. Clients may have catheters, bandages, or diapers that present some highly interesting olfactory stimulation for dogs. Health-care settings have trash cans and garbage cans in many rooms and hallways that also present unfamiliar smells. Dogs need to be trained to respond to a command such as, "leave it," or an incompatible command such as "heel."

Inappropriate urinating. When some dogs smell urine or other unfamiliar smells, they respond by "marking" the area with urine. Dogs who attempt to urinate in a therapy setting should be corrected immediately. For health and image reasons, this is a behavior problem that needs immediate correction or it may warrant dismissal from the program.

Inappropriate eating. Therapy settings will also be full of tempting things to eat. Dogs should be trained to only eat when given approval by the handler. Client pills that have been dropped on the floor can present a serious problem if eaten by a dog. Therapy dogs must also be under good enough control that they can resist food from client trays or food that has been spilled on clients' laps or shirts.

Stealing. Dogs stealing? Stealing is when you take something that doesn't belong to you without permission. Many clients have stuffed animals or toys and some of those toys look better than the old ones at home. This is another problem for which a dog should be able to respond to the command "leave it."

Behavior around other animals. Therapy dogs should be under good control in the presence of other animals such as other therapy dogs or cats. Many facilities have residential animals, and dogs might need to work in a setting with birds, fish or other small animals.

Assessing and Correcting Behavior Problems

Before addressing a potential behavior problem using behavioral procedures, it is important to rule out health problems. Dogs who are hand-shy may have ear infections or vision problems. Apparent behavior problems can result from neurological problems. Dogs with tapeworms may be hungry. Hungry dogs get in the garbage, and might become more aggressive or pushy in order to get food. Dogs who have orthopedic problems and aging problems such as arthritis may have less patience with clients. If there is any chance that any behavior problem could have a medical cause, veterinary care should be provided immediately.

By the time you are volunteering with your pet, you should have already completed some basic training. There are several acceptable choices for addressing behavior problems in therapy settings. In choosing a method for correcting a behavior problem, both the dog and trainer's temperament and ability should be taken into consideration, as well as the environment in which the problem is occurring.

Animal-assisted therapy should be an activity that is fun for both you and your pet. Training methods should be humane and harsh corrections should be avoided. There are numerous dog training books that provide specific information on correcting behavior problems.

Signs of Stress in Therapy Animals

Therapy settings are stressful places. A good therapy animal handler will learn to recognize the signs and symptoms of stress on his or her animal. The physiological signs of stress apply to therapy dogs and other animals.

Signs of stress may include:
• panting
• pacing

- shedding
- diarrhea/bowel movements
- urination
- licking the lips
- coughing
- sneezing
- turning away/avoiding eye contact
- trembling
- shaking (as though the animal were shaking off water)
- yawning
- sweaty paws
- increased or decreased activity
- scratching
- "spacing out"

When beginning therapy, if animals show signs of stress, it may be a clue that additional training and experience are required to help the animal feel comfortable. When experienced therapy animals show signs of stress, it may be time to take a break. The animal might benefit from a walk or being taken to a quiet location. If the stress lasts over several visits, the animal may need a longer break, even several weeks. Finally, if stress persists, it may be necessary to try a different setting or retire the animal. Therapy work should be fun for handlers, and therapy animals who are not enjoying the work should be given the opportunity to participate in other kinds of activities.

SKILLS FOR THERAPY DOGS

All therapy dogs should have some basic skills. Therapy dogs should be reliable and under control at all times. They should exhibit "good citizen" behaviors in therapy and community settings. In addition to overall good behavior, there are some specific skills that therapy dogs can be taught to maximize their involvement in therapy programs.

Some of the skills for therapy dogs include:
- Go see (a person)
- Let's go (or a similar parting command)

- Shake
- Speak
- Put your head down
- Put your head HERE (handler points to location)
- Give kisses (with both client and facility permission)
- Accept a hug
- Paws up
- Jump up (onto a surface)
- Get off
- Sit
- Down
- Stand
- Sit stay
- Down stay
- Stand stay
- Come front
- Heel (for walking in crowded halls)
- Easy (for taking a treat gently; facility permission and handler's discretion)
- Leave it
- Give it to me
- Take it to _____ (person specified)
- Get it
- Turn around
- Crawl
- Get under or in
- Go potty right here (place specified outside)
- Tug or pull (as in removing a glove)
- Find it

DOING TRICKS WITH YOUR DOG

In therapy settings, tricks can be crowd-pleasers. In classes for therapy dog handlers, handlers can have fun teaching their dogs new tricks. The teaching of tricks brings out creative training qualities in people. Too often, with standard obedience behaviors, handlers have been conditioned to train in a serious, intense manner.

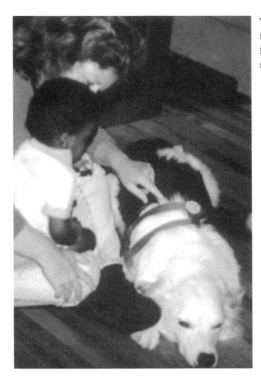

Therapy dogs can be used to teach skills as basic as following simple commands such as "Touch the dog."

Tricks that therapy dogs can learn include behaviors such as bowing, jumping through a hoop, waving good-bye or playing dead. There are a number of books available on how to teach dogs tricks.

SKILLS YOU CAN TEACH USING A THERAPY DOG

There are an unlimited number of activities you can do and skills you can teach using a therapy dog. I developed animal-assisted therapy programs at a facility for people who were developmentally disabled.

I spent more than a month teaching a twelve-year-old boy with profound retardation how to remove a dog biscuit from a box, in order to give a treat to the therapy dog. In the same month, an adult male who was moderately retarded learned to feed and water the resident dog and give a daily heartworm pill with staff supervision. There is a tremendous range of skills that can be taught using a therapy dog.

Therapy dogs can be used to teach skills in a variety of areas:

Cognitive/knowledge
• Dog Breeds: characteristics and history
• Information pertaining to care
• Reading about dogs from a book or magazine

Gross Motor (big muscles—arms and legs)
• Walking the dog
• Throwing a ball for the dog
• Running with the dog

Fine Motor (hands)
• Petting the dog (open fingers)
• Brushing or combing the dog
• Simple grooming tasks
• Holding a leash (for physically impaired clients)
• Filling water dish
• Pouring food
• Feeding the dog a treat (handler decides if appropriate)

Speech/communication
• Giving commands (saying words such as "sit" or "heel")
• Client telling about dogs owned in past
• Socialization with others ("tell Mr. B the story you told me about the dog you had")
• Imitating/giving hand signals (nonverbal communication)
• Describing how dogs make you feel
• Writing or dictating a story about the therapy dog

Daily Living
• Routine care, showing up on time to care for the dog
• Making a purchase for the dog (small treat or toy)

THERAPY DOG CASE STUDIES: LET'S GO FOR A WALK

The following are two case studies in which dogs were used to address problems related to walking. They show how the same behavior (e.g., walking) can be addressed on a very basic level or a more complex level.

1: TEACHING A CHILD TO WALK

Kevin was a three-year-old who had been prenatally exposed to cocaine. He had not yet walked, but he could crawl. His parents were considering purchasing a wheelchair for Kevin, feeling that he would never walk.

A physical therapist had worked closely with us on Kevin's program. She assessed Kevin and felt he had the prerequisite skills for walking and had not walked because he simply wasn't motivated. A ten-step walking program was developed for Kevin wherein he would:

1. Crawl five feet to the dog.
2. With therapist holding one hand and with one hand on porch rail, go six feet to the dog.
3. With one hand on porch rail, go six feet to the dog.
4. Holding therapist's hand only, go across porch six feet to the dog.
5. Standing independently, take one step to the dog.
6. Standing independently, take two steps to the dog.
7. Walk three feet to the dog.
8. Walk five feet to the dog.
9. Walk seven feet to the dog.
10. Walk ten feet to the dog.

The first four steps in the task analysis took ten sessions for Kevin to complete.

In the eleventh session, Kevin was placed standing in the middle of the front porch. The therapy dog, Laddie, and the therapist were about two feet away, with Laddie in a sit-stay. Just as Kevin was instructed, "Come see Laddie," he took his first two independent steps to get to the therapy dog. What a scene: A little boy hugging a dog and laughing, a delighted Border Collie who seemed to know something wonderful had happened and a therapist who sat on the steps and cried. Kevin had all the physical skills and motor abilities for walking. He simply needed some motivation, and he found that motivation in the form of some kisses from a Border Collie.

2: MOTIVATING A WOMAN TO WALK

Michelle was a severely mentally retarded twenty-four-year-old. She could walk, but she did not talk. She made sounds and indicated her preferences by pointing. Michelle lived in a residential facility with sixty other clients.

Michelle attended activities only if staff members took her by the hand and led her to where she needed to go. When she was not in training, she sat in a chair and held a stuffed dog.

The medical staff was concerned because Michelle had a circulation problem. Her feet and legs were swollen and appeared blue much of the time. The physician felt that a walking program was critical for her health.

When the staff attempted to take Michelle for walks, she became aggressive, hitting at them and screaming. I was called to develop a "behavior plan." The first thing I needed to do was find out what Michelle liked (a reinforcer assessment). She did not seem interested in food, drinks or any of the standard reinforcers. Taking a clue from seeing her hold the stuffed dog, I decided to assess the reaction Michelle would have to a therapy dog. Bonnie, a certified therapy Beagle, was called in for a consultation.

After days of hitting at and scratching staff when they tried to get her to walk, Michelle happily jumped out of the chair when I offered her Bonnie's leash. We developed a walking program that gradually increased the distance Michelle needed to walk. We started with fifty feet, then she was taken back to her chair. In a matter of sessions, she was walking a loop around the property with the dog, smiling all the way.

After several weeks, Michelle's circulation improved and she continued to be eager to walk the dog. Michelle was a person for whom the dog was a reinforcer, and she was willing to walk as long as she had a Beagle for a walking partner.

PLANNING FOR FOLLOW-UP

When Michelle's case is described to other therapists, the first question they ask is, "Can you get her to walk without the dog? There won't always be a dog around when she needs to walk for exercise."

In Michelle's case, the dog was the initial reinforcer for the walking program. In addition to the dog, we started pairing other reinforcers with walking. One of the reinforcers included a frosty, cold drink following the walk. Eventually, Michelle would walk with or without the dog.

Once an animal is established as a reinforcer, it is possible to pair the animal with other stimuli so that they eventually have reinforcing properties. Then, if necessary, in order to maximize independence, the animal can be faded.

For clients who are resistive to treatment programs, if animals are reinforcing (i.e., clients like them), therapy dogs can be like a key that unlocks a door. Once the door is open, other things can start to happen with treatment.

GETTING THE RIGHT DOG

As you can see, dogs make excellent therapy animals in the right settings with the right clients. If you don't think the dog you have now is right for whatever reason, but you want to do this kind of work and want to get another or new dog, here are some considerations. One is to adopt a spayed or neutered pet from a shelter. Another is to adopt a spayed or neutered dog from a rescue league. (A rescue league is a group of people affiliated with a particular breed that provides foster homes for abandoned or unwanted dogs until they're adopted.)

If you get a dog from a shelter or rescue league, be sure to check the dog's temperament and get a complete history. Some

Rescue dogs can make excellent therapy dogs. This photo dispels the myth that Greyhounds can't learn to sit. *Courtesy of Cynda Crawford, PhD, DVM*

animals that are turned in at the shelter were given up because they had behavior problems. Many dogs with behavior problems can become wonderful therapy animals if owners are willing to invest some rehabilitative time in the dog.

Some shelter and rescue dogs have a history of biting. These dogs are not appropriate for therapy work. Even though a competent trainer may be able to "fix" a dog who has a history of biting, there is too much at stake in terms of liability to use the animal in a therapy setting. Most insurance companies providing liability insurance for therapy dogs will not consider insuring a dog for therapy work that has a documented history of biting. There are many other fun activities you can do with dogs if therapy work is not an option.

Some of the best therapy dogs I know are rescued Greyhounds—dogs taken from racetracks and adopted into pet homes. So many people believe that Greyhounds are physically structured in a way that makes them unable to sit. Cynda Crawford, PhD, DVM, rescues and trains Greyhounds for obedience competition and therapy work. "It's a myth that Greyhounds can't sit," she says. "They sometimes prefer not to and owners are not willing to teach them new skills. I haven't met one yet that couldn't learn to sit and lay down on command with positive, consistent training."

If you are interested in a purebred dog, another ethical way to obtain a dog is from a responsible breeder. Responsible breeders, unlike "backyard breeders," breed animals to improve a breed, rather than to simply boost their income. Responsible breeders are knowledgeable about breed characteristics and behavior and are interested in hearing from you and helping you if you have problems with your dog.

CHAPTER 4

Cats

For centuries, cats have played an important role in our lives. They have been worshipped and feared and have served as companions and helpers. In recent times, cats have been recognized for their contributions as therapy animals. As early as 3000 B.C., cats were domesticated in Egypt, where they were worshipped as sacred creatures. Eventually, Egyptian cats were used for functional purposes, such as to control rodents.

From Egypt, cats spread throughout Europe. By the Middle Ages, the perception of cats as sacred creatures that should be worshipped had changed. During the Middle Ages people were superstitious, and because many believed that witches could take on a feline form, cats declined in popularity. By the nineteenth century, cats were again popular and were featured in pedigreed cat shows.

The therapeutic benefits of cats have been documented in the literature of animal-assisted therapy. Cats have been used in therapy programs in prisons, nursing homes, schools, hospitals, hospices, AIDS settings and facilities for people with developmental disabilities.

BREED DISPOSITIONS

Are some breeds of cats better for therapy work than others? As with selecting therapy dogs, the most important factor is not breed but whether or not an animal has been raised and socialized properly. If from the time they were kittens cats have a history of positive, frequent interaction with humans, they are more likely to be people-oriented and sociable.

Pat Gonser, PhD, RN, breeds and shows cats. She is nationally recognized for her work using cats in nursing homes. Gonser has worked with Abyssinians and their longhaired counterparts, Somalis. She stresses the importance of early handling and socialization for therapy cats. Her cats enjoy going for walks on harnesses and leashes, they like to interact with people and they play fetch games. Some of Gonser's cats will give a hug or kiss on command. Cats with these kinds of social behaviors can be used to produce the maximum therapeutic results in an animal-assisted therapy setting.

ADVANTAGES AND DISADVANTAGES OF USING CATS

Many people prefer cats over dogs because of their "personalities." Some people seem to prefer an animal that is a little more aloof and less eager to please than a dog usually is. "Dogs don't have the same kind of dignity cats do," I was told by one lady in a nursing home. Appropriate therapy cats (e.g., cats that will lay on someone's lap) provide many chances for nurturing.

Cats are active and playful and can be quite entertaining to watch if they are enjoying playing with a toy. Shorthaired cats require less grooming than some animals. "Lap potato" cats will provide companionship for long periods of time without requiring activity, unlike animals such as dogs. This can be beneficial for people who are inactive and need another living creature to keep them from being alone. When cats are residential animals (e.g., placed in the home of a senior citizen), they require less care than other animals, making ownership easier. For owners who cannot get outside, cats can live indoors. Cats may remind a person of other cats they had as a child.

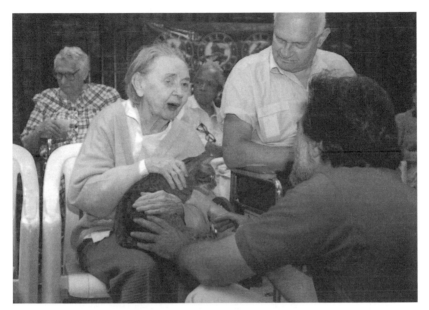

Therapy cats provide many opportunities for nurturing.
Ed Silverman and Jewish Home

One of the disadvantages of using cats in therapy is that some people are highly allergic to cats. Cats typically cannot perform the wide range of skills that dogs can, and if certain behaviors and consistent responses are required of the therapy animal, a dog may be preferred. Compared with small animals such as hamsters and fish, cats require a greater deal of care and management on the part of the animal-assisted therapist. As with any other animal, for some clients, cats will not be the animal of choice.

CAN YOU TRAIN A CAT?

While cats are perceived as not being as trainable as dogs, many people are unaware of the possibilities when it comes to teaching cats new skills. Pat Gonser's cats will go to see a person on command and give hugs and kisses. Few clients expect a cat to do such things, and they respond with amazement and delight.

Scott Hart is an animal trainer who uses operant procedures to train cats. He and his cats have given demonstrations at Delta

Society conferences. By using food as a contingent reinforcer, Hart has trained his cats to follow simple commands and do a wide range of tricks. When you see many of the cats on cat food commercials doing things you were certain cats couldn't do, it's not trick photography. What you're seeing is very often Hart's work, showing that cats can learn a variety of new skills with humane, positive training methods.

Some dog trainers polish their training skills by teaching cats to do "dog things." Some trainers have taught their cats to complete cat-sized agility courses. Cats can learn more than tricks and therapy behaviors. Jon Krueger is a behavior analyst who volunteers his time to animal shelters. To increase their chances of adoption, he teaches good manners to dogs and cats. Krueger uses his feline good citizen training with his own cats at home; they will get on the scales for weighing and follow simple commands.

BEHAVIOR PROBLEMS OF CATS IN THERAPY SETTINGS

Therapy cats might have some behavior problems that will need to be addressed. Many cats, especially males, scent mark areas by spraying urine. Cat breeders recommend neutering as a possible solution to this problem. This is a serious behavior problem that should be remedied immediately if the cat is working in therapy settings. Cats may be wonderful pets who like their owners, but they may not be especially fond of spending time with other people. Hopefully, screening prior to certification will diagnose this problem. If not, cats who are not interested in people may be expressing a preference that should be listened to. Cats might also engage in aggressive behavior (e.g., scratching) if they are agitated. Aggression is a serious problem and is not acceptable in therapy settings.

If your cat has a behavior problem, do not use the animal-assisted therapy setting as a place for training and rehabilitating your cat. You will need to set up situations at home in order to correct problems. Cats (and other animals) who go to therapy settings with you as a volunteer should be under good behavioral control.

Therapy cats should have good manners and skills, such as being able to stay in place.
Courtesy Delta Society, Dawn Haney and George

SKILLS FOR THERAPY CATS

Cats that go to therapeutic settings with you should be well-behaved and under control at all times. Therapy cats should have some very basic skills, such as tolerating petting. In addition to basic skills, you can have a lot of fun volunteering if your cat has been taught some skills that are more advanced. A list of skills for cats in therapy settings includes:

- Walking on harness/leash
- Tolerating being carried through halls and/or crowds
- Accepting traveling in a carrier (in the car)
- Allowing petting by another person (while you hold the cat)
- Allowing another person to hold in lap
- Staying beside another person for petting
- Playing with toy in therapy setting
- Playing with a client and toy in therapy setting
- Going to see another person when called
- Tolerating hugs

- Tolerating being held by a client (to client's chest)
- Giving hugs (places face on client's face)
- Giving kisses on command
- Getting a toy and bring it back
- Taking a treat gently (facility permission; handler judgment)
- Standing (on hind feet) when encouraged
- Rolling over
- Getting down or off on command
- Responding to "no" to behaviors such as licking or starting to use claws

SKILLS TO BE LEARNED FROM A THERAPY CAT

There are many skills and activities you can do as a volunteer with a certified therapy cat. A sample of activities follows.

Cognitive/knowledge
- Breed of cats, recalling information
- Information pertaining to cat care
- Reading about cats from books or magazines
- Recalling stories about cats

Gross Motor (big muscles—arms and legs)
- Walking with cats who like to go for walks on harnesses/leashes
- Reaching out arms to take cat in lap
- Throwing a toy to cat
- Swinging arm at dangling cat toy

Fine Motor (hands)
- Brushing/combing cat
- Petting cat (open fingers) for improving mobility and tactile stimulation
- Holding leash, helping with harness
- Filling water dish

- Pouring food (if appropriate)
- Feeding treat (handler preference; facility permission)
- Holding toys, moving toys to play with cat

Speech/communication
- Talking to cat
- Telling about cats owned
- Describing thoughts/feelings related to therapy cats
- Writing or dictating a story about cats
- Socialization—telling another person about the cat, using pictures

Daily Living
- Routine care of cats, showing up on time for routines
- Making a small purchase in a store if appropriate (cat food, toy, etc.)

WHERE TO GET A CAT FOR THERAPY WORK

If you do not already have a cat, or you know yours wouldn't be suitable for therapy work, yet you want to become involved with a cat, the ethical options for obtaining a cat are similar to those of getting a dog. You can get a spayed or neutered cat from a shelter. However, be aware that many shelter kittens were not properly socialized or handled and they will not be good therapy animals. Adult shelter cats are often turned in for a reason; while a shelter cat may bond to you and be a wonderful pet, it may not be suitable for therapy. Many animal-assisted therapists who work with cats say that, in general, shelter cats do not make good therapy animals. There are exceptions to every rule, however, and some shelter cats have won national therapy cat awards. If you choose to get a cat from the shelter, and you plan to use it for therapy work, be sure that you look very closely at the cat's temperament.

Another ethical source of obtaining a cat is through a responsible breeder. There are over a hundred different cat breeds, and you can learn about breeds by reading one of the many comprehensive books on cats that are available. As with dogs, responsible cat breeders care about their cats. They carefully screen potential owners and assume responsibility for the cat if the owners cannot keep it.

Responsible breeders are knowledgeable about cat breeds and the problems that can affect certain breeds. Many people are aware that certain dog breeds may have hip or other degenerative problems. Fewer people are aware that there are some cat breeds for which aggression and unpredictability are frequently occurring problems. Responsible breeders can help select a cat with a good temperament.

THERAPY CAT CASE STUDY: A CALICO CAT AND VOLUNTEER HELP A THERAPIST

The following case was referred to me for behavioral treatment in the context of my job as a Certified Behavior Analyst. The intervention eventually involved the use of an animal-assisted therapy volunteer and a calico therapy cat.

Vicki was a four-year-old with curly blond hair and blue eyes. She was such a physically beautiful child, it was hard to believe she could cause so much trouble. Vicki was referred for behavioral treatment because she was noncompliant (she would not follow instructions most of the time) and severely aggressive.

Vicki had bitten her infant brother on several occasions. Some of the bites were serious enough to warrant medical treatment at a hospital. In addition to aggression toward her brother, Vicki had attempted to injure animals. Vicki's primary target for aggression toward animals was the family cat.

Understanding the Causes of Animal Abuse

Understanding the causes of animal abuse will help a therapist determine an appropriate treatment. Animal abuse can have several causes.

Psychopathological. Some children who engage in such aggression have serious psychological problems and intensive treatment is needed. Many of these children will be institutionalized or will be in special programs. It is unlikely you will see children in this category of severe emotional disturbance as a volunteer.

Developmental. There is a period in child development where young children enjoy being able to cause a reaction in their world. When very young children are given towers made of blocks, the most fun activity is knocking the blocks over. Many young children enjoy throwing things off high-chair tables. When a young child holds a kitten and gives it a light squeeze, the kitten may make a noise. "Squeeze this thing and it says 'Meow'" can be an entertaining idea to a young child. At this age, there is no understanding of the concept of harming the animal.

Social. In social psychology, there is something called a contagion effect, as in the word contagious. Sometimes, children in groups, especially preteens and teenagers, will participate in animal abuse as part of gaining peer acceptance. We did a project in a petting zoo where older children were being rough with animals. After we provided training, children behaved appropriately. When new children arrived and were loud and overly active as they visited the enclosures, the effects of training disappeared with the children who had received training.

Environmental. In cases where children are in abusive environments, they often learn to abuse others. Too often, human services professionals see families where dad hits mom, mom hits the children and the children abuse the pets.

Educational. Sometimes children abuse animals because they simply have not been taught how to interact appropriately with them. A child might throw a geriatric animal in a swimming pool, thinking that it really would enjoy swimming on a hot summer day. Children may lack the skills needed to interact with an animal in an appropriate manner, such as how to pet a cat nicely.

In Vicki's case, it was suspected that a main cause for the abuse was *educational*—she had not been taught a different standard of behavior. A behavior diagnostic assessment and functional analysis of the problem indicated that her parents had actually shaped and were reinforcing aggressive and abusive behavior. Vicki's parents were low-income and neither of the young parents had completed high school.

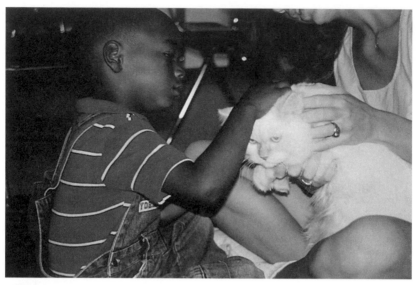

Children can be taught to interact with cats in an appropriate manner.
Delight Hicks

In the initial observations, when Vicki would engage in minor aggression (like shoving a sibling who was a toddler or pulling the cat's tail) her parents would smile and laugh, saying things like, "Ooh, she's so mean." Sometimes the father would say, "You wanna be mean—come try it with me." A game of rough play would ensue where Vicki would have fun and laugh.

As an immediate intervention, both parents were required (by state agencies) to have regular parent training and behavior management sessions in the home. At the same time, behavioral training began in the home to teach Vicki to interact appropriately with her siblings.

In part of the parent training relating to animal abuse, both parents were taught that young children should not be left unsupervised with animals. The parents had to sign a treatment plan contract agreeing that they would supervise all interactions between Vicki, her siblings and animals.

Further, to prevent any further abuse of the family cat, I decided to teach Vicki to interact with the cat in an appropriate manner (to pet the cat nicely). There was only one problem with this great idea. The problem was the cat wanted no part of interacting nicely with Vicki. I couldn't say that I blamed the cat. I also didn't feel that the cat would be safe and reliable in a regular training program.

The bottom line regarding the safety and care of your animal in animal-assisted therapy is *never* put your animal in a position where you suspect it may be harmed.

In Vicki's program, because there was a chance that she might be aggressive toward any animal that we brought in, I started the treatment using a stuffed cat that looked remarkably like the family's calico cat. Vicki was taught to respond to the command, "Easy." Compliance (which was one of the original problems causing the referral) was addressed by instructing Vicki to pet specific areas of the cat: "Pet his tummy." She was often given physical guidance; that is, the therapist would hold her hand to guide the petting. Vicki was praised for appropriate petting. "That's so nice, you are being very gentle." She was reinforced with praise and cookies following each short session. Vicki's parents were trained to give praise during the program.

Vicki had learned to nicely pet the stuffed cat. Would the results generalize to a real cat? A volunteer with a therapy cat started coming to the sessions. In the first few sessions, there were a few practice trials with the stuffed animal. Appropriate petting was reinforced and then Vicki was given the chance to pet the real cat. The results generalized quickly to the therapy cat. Within several months, Vicki also interacted nicely with the family cat and a neighbor's puppies.

As a result of a systematic plan to teach kindness to animals, Vicki's parents learned an important lesson about the dangers of tolerating even the most simple form of animal mistreatment. Vicki was a kinder child, and the last time I saw the family cat, he was sitting in Vicki's lap purring.

The progress and generalization that occurred in this intervention could not have been made had we not had access to a therapy cat with good temperament. A cat was needed that would tolerate being placed in a child's lap and stay there while someone guided the child's hands during petting. This case study also shows the important role a volunteer with a therapy cat can have in helping a therapist achieve treatment plan goals.

As a volunteer with a therapy cat, you have the chance to make valuable contributions in animal-assisted therapy settings.

CHAPTER 5

Horses

As early as 500 B.C., the Greeks gave horseback rides to people who were considered untreatable in order to improve their morale. Medical literature from the eighteenth and nineteenth centuries describes the therapeutic benefits of horseback riding.

In 1870, in Paris, Chassigne conducted one of the first studies documenting the benefits of horses in therapy programs. He described the many improvements a client could have in posture, balance and muscle control as a result of riding horses.

In the 1960s therapists in the United States, Great Britain and Germany were using horses in therapy programs. Today, about thirty countries have therapeutic riding programs. There are therapeutic riding associations, certifications, training and standards and international congresses.

USES OF HORSES IN THERAPY PROGRAMS

There are three primary ways in which horses are used in therapy programs. First, therapeutic riding can be an adapted recreational sport for people with disabilities and special needs. This is basically horseback riding for fun, though there may be some

Balance, mobility and coordination can be improved through remedial riding exercises.
Courtesy Delta Society

additional benefits for the rider, including improved psychological well-being. People with disabilities preventing them from sitting in a saddle can participate in recreational riding by driving horse-drawn carts or wagons.

A second type of therapeutic riding is remedial riding, where therapeutic goals and objectives are incorporated into the riding program. Goals can be behavioral or physical in nature. An example of a goal in a remedial riding program would be to improve the sitting balance of a child with cerebral palsy.

The third type of therapeutic riding is referred to as "hippotherapy." The term hippotherapy comes from the Greek word *eohippos,* which means horse. Hippotherapy is done by qualified, trained professionals who know about horses and a particular field such as occupational or physical therapy. Hippotherapy goals include improving posture, balance, strength and mobility.

SCREENING HORSES FOR THERAPY WORK

It is important that horses used in therapy programs have sound conformation (good builds) because they will be required to perform very controlled movements for extended periods of time. All of the body parts of a potential therapy horse should be evaluated for conformation, including the head, neck, withers, back, croup, hindquarters, hocks, feet, pasterns, stifle, forelegs, shoulders and chest.

Horses should also be evaluated in terms of behavior and skills. Therapy horses should be reliable and predictable. They should tolerate being led and having assistants walk at their sides. Therapy horses should have a repertoire of commands that they will follow, such as "Walk forward," and "Whoa." The horse should behave appropriately when the rider changes positions. Position changes include mounting, dismounting or changing position in the saddle. Depending on the disabilities of the rider, therapy horses have to tolerate different movements from different riders; some riders slide down the horse's body to dismount, others are lifted onto and off of the horse.

A detailed screening procedure for therapy horses is described by Jan Spink in the book, *Developmental Riding Therapy: A Team Approach to Assessment and Treatment* (Therapy Skill Builders, 1993). Additional information on working with therapy horses can be obtained from the North American Riding for the Handicapped Association (NARHA). When horses are used in therapy work, it is important that they receive comprehensive screening.

GETTING INVOLVED WITHOUT A HORSE

If you would like to work with horses in animal-assisted therapy and your own horse does not qualify, you can volunteer your services to help others with therapeutic riding programs. You could assist by being a "sidewalker," a person who walks at the side of the horse to ensure the client is safe. You could be the person who leads the horse, or assists the client in mounting or dismounting. If you are a highly skilled rider with teaching experience, you might volunteer to teach others in therapeutic riding settings.

HORSES TO VISIT

Some volunteers have horses that are calm and predictable, but not necessarily suitable for riding. If you have such a horse, you might volunteer to have your horse visited. For children (or adults) who have never had contact with a horse, a trip to the barn to simply pet a horse can be thrilling.

In therapeutic riding programs, volunteers are needed as leaders and sidewalkers. This horse is Rocky, winner of the 1988 Delta Society Therapy Horse Award, part of SPUR (Special People United to Ride). *Courtesy Delta Society*

ADVANTAGES AND DISADVANTAGES OF USING HORSES

Horses can be used to work on physical skills in a way not possible with other animals. They can be used to address goals related to balance, posture, strength, mobility and coordination. Many people love horses but have not had many opportunities to interact with them. The self-confidence that can be gained from being able to control an animal as large as a horse is tremendous. Autistic children who engage in self-stimulatory behaviors such as rocking will frequently stop self-stimulating when on a horse. For many people, the idea of riding a horse is magical.

Appropriate therapy horses may be hard to find. Many staff and administrators will be nervous about clients on an animal as big as a horse, so the program may be hard to sell. Some people are allergic to horses. If horses go visiting, a suitably large space is needed and a great deal of clean-up (getting rid of manure) may be required. If clients come to where the horse is stabled, transportation may be a problem for regular visits. In addition to the horse's owner, it may be necessary to have sidewalkers and a leader for safety reasons. This means that animal-assisted therapy using horses can be very labor and resource intensive. Some clients will be afraid of horses, some will need special equipment for riding. Unless the program is a large, organized riding program, special equipment may not be available.

WHICH BREEDS ARE BEST?

In general, people think of thoroughbred horses as high-strung and highly spirited. This would mean that thoroughbreds would not be suitable therapy horses. This may be true, but as with other species, there are exceptions to every rule. If a thoroughbred has been handled from birth for the purpose of being sociable and provided with consistent, humane training, it may be behaviorally acceptable for therapy work.

The primary things that should be considered in matching horses and clients in therapy programs are the horse's temperament, size and body parts (e.g., for this rider the horse's back is too narrow) and whether or not the horse has a gait that is appropriate for the client.

WHAT HORSES CAN DO IN THERAPY

Horses can be directly used to improve physical skills more than any other therapy animals. In addition to physical skills, clients can learn cognitive and social skills in animal-assisted therapy that involves horses. Skills can be as simple as reaching out to pet a horse or as complex as advanced dressage routines.

Cognitive/knowledge
- Recognizing types of horses
- Learning the names of body parts
- Learning the types of equipment

Therapy horses can be used to teach basic skills to children with disabilities.
Delta Society

• Knowing different gaits
• Memorizing patterns for basic dressage
• Knowing meaning of commands

Gross Motor (big muscles—arms and legs)
• Mounting—lifting leg over the saddle
• Dismounting—swinging leg down
• Putting foot in stirrup

Fine motor (hands)
• Fastening buckles, tying ropes
• Brushing the horse
• Holding the reins
• Holding on to a saddle
• Opening contracted hands

Balance and trunk control
• Bending forward as instructed
• Leaning back as instructed
• Sitting up straight
• Holding head up straight
• Holding reins and balancing (without holding onto the saddle)
• Coordination—one foot in stirrup, other leg over saddle

Self-esteem
• Boosting self-esteem and self-confidence (ability to control an animal as large as a horse can give a client an instant boost in self-confidence)

THERAPY HORSE CASE STUDY: ACTIVITIES OF A THERAPY HORSE AND VOLUNTEER

Connie Stone and her paint/thoroughbred cross, Lucy, were the first registered therapy horse team in the Delta Society Pet

Partners Program. Stone and Lucy work with children, a women's shelter, and retired farmers and cowboys in a Colorado nursing home. Lucy's greatest strengths as a therapy horse are her good manners and calm, unflappable nature. But Stone says that no matter how calm a horse is, you never know if something may startle it. She always requires that another adult be present with her on visits to supervise clients or to hold the horse. Stone feels that one person can't do everything that needs to be done on a therapy horse visit, and having the assistance of a volunteer is essential.

THERAPY HORSE CASE STUDY: RIDING CALMS AN AGGRESSIVE MAN

Dean was a twenty-two-year-old client who had a head injury. When he was seven years old, he fell from his bunk bed to the floor in the middle of the night. Later the same night, he began seizuring and his life and the lives of his family members changed forever. Neurological problems, learning problems and severe behavior problems that followed the injury resulted in Dean spending the rest of his childhood years in special programs. By the time he was twenty-two, Dean was severely aggressive. He had no impulse control and was considered a danger to others. He was institutionalized and, because he had caused injuries to several staff that required them to be hospitalized, he spent much of his time in restraints. Dean's parents were strong advocates and they were persistent in insisting that he receive treatment for his behavior problems.

When behavioral treatment began, Dean was restrained much of the time. Over many months of behavioral treatment, there was some progress and some activities were introduced to reintroduce Dean to the outside world. Dean expressed an interest in animals. Because he had gone so long without being touched or touching any other living thing in an acceptable way, animal-assisted therapy seemed to be a good intervention for Dean.

Unfortunately, even though he had made some progress, Dean was still somewhat unpredictable with regard to his anger. For that reason, smaller animals such as dogs, kittens, gerbils and birds were not appropriate for Dean's animal-assisted therapy program.

After carefully assessing Dean's behavior and physical abilities, it was decided that only one animal would be suitable for him, and that was a horse. A volunteer with a therapy horse began working with professionals from the facility where Dean lived. A behavior plan was developed and Dean would get a chance to ride the horse if he had met the program requirements. Initially, he had to go one day without an aggressive outburst, then two, then three. If there was an aggressive incident on the day horseback riding was planned, the activity would be canceled.

Several staff members accompanied Dean on all of the visits to ride the horse to ensure that in the event of an aggressive outburst, enough people were available to prevent an injury to any person or the horse. Dean respected the horse. In the entire course of treatment, he never once attempted to hit, kick or engage in any aggressive act toward the horse. On several occasions, Dean did engage in inappropriate behavior. He got on the horse and began acting like he was going to fall off. He was acting silly and attempting to get attention.

Dean's horseback riding represents another case where, without the volunteer and her horse, the program would not have been possible. In Dean's case, the horse was the perfect therapy animal. In addition to improving balance and physical strength, the horse gave Dean a means to have contact with another living creature. Riding the horse also boosted Dean's self-esteem. Because of his head injury, Dean couldn't walk without problems. He couldn't run without problems. His speech was difficult to understand. But when he rode the horse, things were different. Dean knew that riding a horse was not easy. Sitting tall in the saddle, he thought about his abilities, not his disabilities.

CHAPTER 6

Farm Animals

FARM ANIMALS AS THERAPISTS

Throughout history, people have had domesticated farm animals. While some were consumed as food or used for wool, many early farmers cared for and showed affection for their animals. Some of the first animal-assisted therapy programs involved the use of farm animals. In the ninth century, a therapeutic program using farm animals was established in Gheel, Belgium.

I visited the program in Gheel several years ago. While some things have changed in Gheel over the centuries, many things have not. People with disabilities are still placed in the homes of farmers, and a major part of the treatment process involves learning to live on a farm and work with farm animals. For centuries, the Gheel program has taught people vocational skills and how to be independent. Caring for other living things is learned at Gheel by working with farm animals. Gheel is a program that has stood the test of time.

Another farm program that has stood the test of time is Bethel, in Bielefeld, Germany. Bethel started in 1867 and continues today as a program for people with disabilities. Farm animals are involved in much of the therapy and the program now has over 5,000 clients and 5,000 staff.

A MODERN MODEL FARM PROGRAM

At a farm about an hour from New York City, 102 children between the ages of six and eighteen learn valuable lessons from farm animals. The farm is Green Chimneys, located in Brewster, New York. Sam Ross, PhD, is the executive director of Green Chimneys. He opened the facility as a boarding school in 1948. In recent years the program has served children with emotional and psychological problems. Many of Green Chimneys' students failed at several other programs before being placed at Green Chimneys for residential treatment.

The Green Chimneys farm is on 150 acres, and almost 400 animals are available to provide therapy and companionship. Green Chimneys has a therapeutic riding program and a wildlife rehabilitation center, where students are taught to rehabilitate animals such as foxes and birds of prey. Some children who come to Green Chimneys have never seen a live farm animal.

Students at Green Chimneys live in houses that are staffed around-the-clock, and many of the homes have a resident dog or cat. Each child at Green Chimneys is responsible for taking care of at least one animal; some children care for larger animals and others care for smaller pets. Green Chimneys has a breeding program for rare breeds such as shaggy, red Highland cattle. These rare breeds fit right into a program where everyone is unique. Green Chimneys' students have different preferences in the types of animals they relate to—one student prefers a large pig while another believes that a ferret is the neatest animal in the whole place.

Green Chimneys has developed an outreach program called "Farm on the Moo-ve." In this program farm animals are taken to the city to visit with people who would otherwise be unable to get to a farm. For more information on Green Chimneys, contact: **Green Chimneys,** Putnam Lake Road, Box 719, Brewster, NY 10509.

Farm animals can teach children kindness and respect for other living things.
Courtesy of Omerod-England and Delta Society

THE BENEFITS OF FARM ANIMALS

Sam Ross is an internationally recognized consultant for farm programs. For years, he has seen the wide range of benefits that farm animals can provide in therapy programs. Farm animals can have calming effects, such as when a child goes to the barn to tell their secrets to the donkey. Many of the children at Green Chimneys have had bad experiences with adults, and caring for the farm animals is an enjoyable activity that children and adults can do together. Farm animals can be used to teach important life lessons, such as self-worth, responsibility and how to care for another living thing. When Green Chimneys' students graduate and leave the program, many may never own a cow or chicken.

But if, when they become parents, they treat their children with kindness and respect, the Green Chimneys farm program was successful.

SCREENING FARM ANIMALS FOR THERAPY WORK

Farm animals used in animal-assisted therapy can include cows, sheep, goats, pigs, chickens, turkeys, ducks and donkeys. Believe it or not, there are actually some registered therapy chickens!

As with other animals, all farm animals that are to be used in animal-assisted therapy should have a complete veterinary check and a clean bill of health. Animals should be up-to-date on all vaccines and relevant immunizations for the species and geographical area. Farm animals that will be used in situations where clients will have direct contact with the animals should be temperament tested. As a part of the temperament testing, therapy visits should be simulated. Any animals that are nervous or unpredictable should not be used for animal-assisted therapy. If temperament is questionable, clients could participate in farm activities that do not involve going in or near the animal enclosures. However, on a long-term basis, to achieve maximum benefits from therapy, there should be contact with the animals. If animals at one location are not suitable, it might be necessary to find another farm.

ADVANTAGES AND DISADVANTAGES OF USING FARM ANIMALS IN THERAPY

Farm animals can give clients a sense of competence that can only be gained by working with larger animals. Smaller farm animals such as chickens and ducks are preferred by clients who do not wish to have intense interaction with an animal, like the kind a dog would require. Some people like farm animals and farms. Farm animals provide therapeutic benefits that come from caring for other living things. Daily chores related to caring for farm animals can teach responsibility. Tasks related to farm animal care

To achieve maximum benefits, there should be opportunities for contact with farm animals.
Delta Society

(such as cleaning a stall) are real tasks that give a sense of accomplishment. For appropriate clients, many of the jobs involved in farm animal care can be developed into meaningful vocational skills (e.g., the client might get a job in a dairy farm).

There are some disadvantages to using farm animals in animal-assisted therapy. Very few programs are equipped to keep farm animals. If programs cannot have residential farm animals, clients must be taken to a farm to work with the animals. Transportation is often a problem in therapy settings. Farm animals are expensive to purchase and care for. Farm animals are large and some staff members may fear that clients will be harmed around animals. If there is an incident and someone is hurt by a large farm animal, there is a good chance the injury will be more severe than an injury caused by a small animal. In general, farm animals are more difficult to train and more unpredictable than other animals that could be used in therapy. Programs involving farm animals require adequate staff or volunteer support; single volunteers need assistance. When and where farm animals eliminate is not always controllable. Large animals require a great deal of clean-up if they are visiting. Sometimes staff are offended if smaller animals (such as ducks) eliminate during a visit.

SKILLS YOU CAN TEACH USING FARM ANIMALS

Cognitive/knowledge
• Names of species
• Information on species care
• Measuring food
• Time concepts—feeding schedules

Gross Motor (big muscles—arms and legs)
• Shoveling manure
• Sweeping
• Raking
• Carrying buckets and food pails

Fine Motor (hands)
• Brushing coat (if appropriate)
• Picking up eggs
• Pouring food
• Scooping oats
• Milking cows

Speech/communication
• Telling how animals make you feel
• Telling another person about your animal (socialization)
• Writing/dictating a story about the animal(s)
• Reporting animal's status to supervisor

Daily Living
- Responsibility
- Being on time
- Being consistent—e.g., showing up every morning at 6 a.m.
- Administering routine treatments
- Following a schedule (feeding)

Vocational skills
- Dairy work
- Working on a goat farm
- Working at a stable with horses (related tasks—cleaning stalls, etc.)

FARM ANIMAL CASE STUDY: A CHICKEN BREAKS THROUGH TO A LITTLE GIRL

Lorie was a five-year-old who was referred for behavioral treatment because she was electively mute. Elective mutism is a condition where children choose not to talk even though they have the ability to talk. Children who are sexually or physically abused may become electively mute, as can children who are having trouble coping with something in their lives.

Lorie was attending a preschool program when I first saw her. To my dismay, on my first consulting visit, in Lorie's presence, the teacher said, "She won't talk; no matter what you do, she isn't going to talk." In a play area, I sat on the floor near Lorie and played with toys, describing what I was doing. "I think my doll will ride in the car now," I said, never prompting Lorie to talk. As I played near Lorie, several other children came over and said, "Don't talk to her, she can't talk."

Lorie's records indicated she had not spoken a single word outside of her home setting in over a year and a half. After a complete evaluation, I decided that Lorie needed a fresh start. Based on my recommendations, she was transferred to another preschool program. In the new program, Lorie had a wonderful teacher. The first time a child said, "She can't talk," Lorie's eyes widened and she watched to see how the teacher would respond. "She can talk," said the teacher, "right now, she's just making a choice not to."

We developed a fourteen-step plan for treating Lorie's elective mutism. Within days, Lorie was talking to other children in play situations. Within a few weeks she was talking in one-word responses to the familiar adults in the classroom. We then began to work on having Lorie talk with adults other than those in her classroom. Lorie's favorite staff person was picked up in the afternoons by her husband. Every afternoon he would greet Lorie. For months, he got no response.

One day, Lorie went home with the staff member. Her husband came home from work and tried to talk with Lorie. She did not respond. In frustration, he finally said, "I'm going outside to feed the chickens. You can come if you want." Inside the chicken coop, he turned around, and there was Lorie. Smiling, she looked at the hens and the little chicks as they ran about the pen. Suddenly, she ran up and spoke her first words in more than eighteen months to an adult outside of her home, "Can I help?" she asked, obviously excited about feeding the chickens.

For months, we had tried introducing new people to Lorie in her classroom because we thought she might feel more comfortable talking in a safe environment. I never predicted Lorie would start talking to a new adult away from the home or school setting. The mother hen and her chicks were able to stimulate language and break down barriers for a child who was unwilling to speak.

Since working with Lorie I've talked to many other therapists who have abandoned traditional therapy settings in favor of treating children in the presence of animals and nature. We were fortunate to have had a volunteer who offered her farm as a place Lorie could visit. As a therapist, one of my most valuable lessons about the treatment of elective mutism was learned in a barnyard.

CHAPTER 7

Other Animals

OTHER ANIMALS AS THERAPISTS

Smaller and less commonly seen animals have had a place in the history of animal-assisted therapy. In the 1790s, the York Retreat started in Yorkshire, England. The York Retreat was founded by the Society of Friends with the encouragement of William Tuke. Tuke was a Quaker tea merchant who was appalled at the treatment of patients in asylums. He convinced a physician to work with him and his friends to establish a program for teaching patients to care for a variety of small animals such as rabbits.

In the 1940s, soldiers in the Army Air Corps Hospital in Pawling, New York, had a therapy program that involved interaction with snakes, frogs, turtles and other small animals. The animals were used to take the patients' minds off the war.

Even though smaller and less common animals such as llamas are not as popular as other therapy animals, their effects in therapy programs can be dramatic.

Other animals used in animal-assisted therapy settings may include birds, fish, hamsters, gerbils, guinea pigs, rabbits and llamas.

The benefits of smaller animals such as birds and fish are being recognized in therapy settings.

Birds

Cats and dogs aren't the only ones flocking to therapy settings with volunteers! Birds of all types are volunteering with their humans. Therapy birds include parrots, macaws, cockatiels and parakeets. The San Francisco SPCA had a therapy rooster named "Elvis." Elvis was rescued from cockfighting and, after he was rehabilitated, visited sick and isolated people and school children.

For a long time, we have known that birds can be trained to perform simple tasks and to talk. Now it looks like birds are smarter than we thought. Irene Pepperberg, PhD, an ethologist, has worked for years with an African Grey parrot named Alex. Alex can correctly identify numbers of objects, shapes and colors. Pepperberg is estimating the cognitive power of parrots as somewhere in the range of a human five-year-old, and their emotional development as equivalent to a three-year-old.

Some therapy birds will not yet be ready to graduate from elementary school, but many birds can be trained to have good manners and a basic level of skills for therapy work. Therapy

Birds can provide stimulation, entertainment and companionship.

birds should be able to perform many of the behaviors on the Canine Good Citizen Test in a modified form. (Would this be the Avian Good Citizen Test?) In therapy settings, birds should be able to be walked through a crowd and they should tolerate noisy distractions. When placed near a client, birds who are tame enough to be removed from cages should stay in place. The best birds for therapy are those that have been handled and raised by a reputable breeder.

Some residential settings might have smaller caged birds such as finches. Even though these birds are under no behavioral control, they can provide clients with a great deal of stimulation, entertainment and companionship.

Fish

As a volunteer, it is unlikely that you will take fish to visit therapy settings. On an ongoing basis, this would be neither practical nor humane treatment for fish. However, if you are a volunteer who knows about fish and you have interest in aquariums, you might want to offer to maintain an aquarium at a facility or assist a designated facility staff person in teaching appropriate clients to care for fish.

Some fish, such as Red Oscars, have interesting personalities. They learn to watch people and will follow the movement of some people. Research shows that watching fish in an aquarium can have a calming effect on people. It is for this reason that so many physicians' and dentists' waiting rooms have fish tanks.

Hamsters

All hamsters in the United States descended from the same Old World hamster family: a female and her twelve young that were captured in Syria in 1930. Hamsters are members of the rodent family. They have cheek pouches to carry food. The most common pet hamsters are Golden Hamsters. Their life span is one to three years, and they are nocturnal, meaning that they will often sleep during the day and become active at night. Hamsters that will be handled by others should be handled regularly in order to maintain tameness. Hamsters should be handled carefully in therapy settings because, if startled, they may bite. If clients have unpredictable movements, hamsters may not be the therapy animal of choice.

Hamsters are known for their abilities to escape from cages, so hamster housing must pass security inspections! Hamsters should be housed alone to prevent unplanned breeding. Hamster litters can have as many as eighteen offspring; unless you have eighteen *really good* friends, it is not a wise idea to allow hamsters to breed.

A product is available called the Hamster Habitat™, which is a series of interconnecting clear tubes that lead to a hamster cage. This type of housing would permit clients in a therapy setting to watch the hamsters move from place to place. As with fish and some other small animals, volunteers who enjoy hamsters could volunteer to help care for a residential hamster at a facility.

GERBILS

Gerbils are also rodents, and they originally came from Africa and Asia. Gerbils have elongated rear legs and long tails. The most popular gerbil in America is the Mongolian Gerbil. Gerbils are similar to hamsters, and the same precautions and advantages apply to them as to their larger cousins. They should not be placed in drafts and they can be stressed by loud noises and fast movements.

GUINEA PIGS

Many people who use small animals for animal-assisted therapy vote for guinea pigs as the animals "most likely to succeed." They are perhaps the most popular residential pets. Like hamsters and gerbils, guinea pigs are rodents.

Guinea pigs are native to South America where, for centuries, they were used as a food source in Peru. At ten to fourteen inches long, guinea pigs are larger than hamsters and gerbils. They have an average life span of three to five years, but they can live as long as eight years. Guinea pigs urinate frequently, so in therapy settings it is best to present them in a basket or on a towel. Guinea pigs also have nails that can cause scratches, another reason for not having clients hold the animals without protection. There are some special dietary requirements for guinea pigs: They require vitamin C, which can be provided in guinea pig pellets.

RABBITS

Rabbits can make good residential pets if an indoor hutch and regular caretaker are available. Rabbits can dig under fences, so outside enclosures and exercise yards should be secure. Rabbits are especially good animals for tactile activities such as petting soft fur.

Rabbits are curious and affectionate, and they respond to attention and interaction. Some rabbits like to be held, but many will do better in therapy settings if they are presented to clients in a

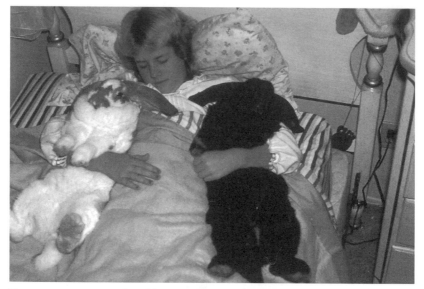

Temperament-sound rabbits make excellent therapy animals if they are properly socialized.
Courtesy of Delta Society

basket. Rabbits can be trained to use a litter box, and they like having a cage where they can feel safe and secure.

Rabbits should not be left unsupervised because they can chew through computer cords or phone wires. A strange habit for a rabbit, you say? Not really. Bunnies in the wild chew through vines to mark paths, and the behavior seems to generalize to home appliance cords and computers. Rabbits should be neutered or spayed. Neutering can help with behavior changes that occur at sexual maturity, such as mood swings, aggressive behavior and scent marking. Temperament-sound rabbits can make excellent therapy animals if they are properly socialized. More than one owner of a personable rabbit has told me, "You're nobody 'til some bunny loves you."

LLAMAS

The llama is a South American member of the camel family. Llamas stand about four feet high at the shoulders and are covered with a fine, long wool. Llamas were domesticated as wool and pack animals more than 4,000 years ago by the Indians of Peru.

Llamas are more popular in some parts of the country than in others. In places where llamas are popular they are kept as pets and pack animals. Some resorts in the western United States have added "llama trekking" as a featured activity. In llama trekking, llamas carry the packs and provisions of hikers to their scenic picnic or camp sites. Each person is assigned a llama that they lead on the trek. Many resort llamas have pack animal personalities; they do their jobs and carry packs but prefer not to get friendly with visitors. They may shy away or resist petting and affection.

Llamas have also been introduced to animal-assisted therapy. No other animal in therapy settings looks or feels quite like a llama. In 1989, Jack and Donna Moore had taken llamas on fifty-two visits to nursing homes and other facilities.

In the Fall 1989 *Llamas Magazine*, the Moores provided some guidelines for taking llamas on therapy visits. The guidelines suggested by the Moores included the following: Llamas that are taken on visits should be "potty trained"; at least two handlers should be present on all visits; llamas that visit should be desensitized to wheelchairs and other health-care equipment; llamas need a break about every hour and be sure you know if the llama you are taking on a visit tolerates loud noises.

Llamas will meet and greet new people by sniffing them, so a lesson in llama habits may be beneficial for all clients the first time a llama comes to a facility.

SCREENING OTHER ANIMALS

The animals described in this chapter are no different than other animals in that they need to be screened for therapy work. Screening includes a complete veterinary screening, temperament testing and behavioral observations. Prior to visits it is important to determine how each individual animal should be handled. Volunteers should have visited the setting without the animal, and screening should include a realistic simulation of a therapy visit. For small animals that visit in cages, screening can be conducted with modified behavior tests, such as the animal being walked through a crowd in a cage.

ADVANTAGES OF SMALL OR LESS COMMON ANIMALS

The animals in this category that are presented in cages or baskets are smaller and easier to manage. Smaller animals require less care and clients can learn the skills needed to care for a small pet quicker than they can a larger one. Smaller animals are inexpensive to feed and people are generally not afraid of them.

Small animals can provide a special kind of passive therapy. Clients can benefit from small animal contact simply by watching the animals. If a facility decides that clients may have animals, it is practical for more than one client to have a small animal such as a bird or fish. It is more difficult to manage larger numbers of bigger pets like dogs and cats.

The llama is the "less common" animal in this group, and is not considered a small animal. Advantages of llamas are that they are so very different, they usually get a reaction from almost everyone. Llamas provide a tactile (touch) experience that other animals do not. In facilities where everything is the same day after day, llamas provide a stimulating, different kind of experience.

DISADVANTAGES OF SMALL OR LESS COMMON ANIMALS

Smaller animals are generally not as healthy as larger animals. Rabbits can die from getting overheated and birds can become very sick if they are chilled or left in a draft. Smaller animals cannot be as readily handled as larger animals. Smaller animals cannot be trained to have as many reliable skills as a larger animal like a dog. Smaller animals often have short life spans; the death of an animal can be devastating for some clients.

Llamas also have some disadvantages. They require transportation to facilities and at least two volunteers should be present for llama visits. Llamas require a greater amount of clean-up than do smaller animals. Some llamas do not like to be touched, and many llamas do not appear loving and affectionate.

SKILLS YOU CAN TEACH USING SMALL OR LESS COMMON ANIMALS

Cognitive/knowledge
• Learning names of species
• Learning information about species history and care

Gross Motor (big muscles—arms and legs)
• Reaching out to take the animal (can be in basket or cage)
• Walking to a specified place to see animal
• Holding out arm to hold parrot (if appropriate)
• Reaching to touch llama

Fine Motor (hands)
• Controlled movement ("touch the animal right here")
• Feeling the coat of the llama (tactile)
• Stroking the bird's head
• Grasping edge of basket to take guinea pig
• Pouring food
• Getting a pinch of fish food (for food activities, make sure animals are not overfed)

Speech/communication
• Saying words to bird
• Repeating words of bird
• Telling another person about the animal (socialization)

Daily Living
• Responsibility (showing up to care for animal at specified time)
• Cleaning cages

Behavioral

- Access to animal contingent on appropriate behavior

Physiological

- Calming influence—especially fish

CASE STUDY: USING A THERAPY BIRD FOR TREATING BEHAVIOR PROBLEMS

Kevin was a three-year-old who had been prenatally exposed to drugs. He was referred for behavioral treatment because he was not walking or talking and he had severe behavior problems. Kevin had frequent tantrums and became noncompliant during most daily routines. Because his mother had some physical disabilities, Kevin's tantrums were potentially dangerous. During bathing, Kevin would kick, scream and bang his head; on several occasions, he slipped out of his mother's hands in the bathtub.

After weeks of very slow progress, I decided to observe Kevin in a setting outside of the home. I took him to a nearby beach. Some seagulls flew by and Kevin began to smile and point at the birds and make noises. This was the first sign I'd seen of any expressive communication.

Kevin's entire family was receiving services, and he had a teenage sister who had been requesting a pet. With the mother's approval, a cockatiel was purchased for the sister. As I'd hoped, Kevin was fascinated with the bird. On the seventh home visit, Kevin looked at his mother and said his first word, "Bird." It was clear that the bird was a reinforcer. A program was developed where the bird was used as a contingent reinforcer for bathing.

Initially, if Kevin simply tolerated being placed in the tub with no tantrums, he was immediately pulled out and taken to see the bird. Then, he had to tolerate having his upper body quickly washed. If he did not have a tantrum, he was wrapped in a towel and quickly taken down the hall to see the bird. By the end of the program, Kevin's mother was able to bathe his whole body without a tantrum. Eventually, Kevin was given free access to the bird (with his sister's permission and supervision). A therapy dog was then introduced to work on walking.

There was something about birds that captured Kevin's interest. The bird played a critical role in Kevin's treatment. Kevin was not responsive to traditional reinforcers like hugs, food, juice or toys. The bird elicited some dramatic responses quickly and those responses changed the way Kevin's mother thought about him. When Kevin looked at his mother and said, "Bird," she said, "He can learn to talk." As a result of Kevin's response to the bird, family members began believing he had capabilities for the first time.

CASE STUDY: USING A GERBIL TO TEACH NAPTIME SKILLS

Michael was a five-year-old when he entered a structured pre-school program. He was receiving services because he was emotionally disturbed and having some behavior problems following several years of sexual abuse. Michael was extremely bright, but socially, he was behaving like a much younger child.

As part of the daily schedule in the classroom, children were required to lay on mats and take a nap after lunch. In Michael's class, all of the children slept at naptime. That is, until Michael arrived. During nap, Michael would talk loudly and get toys from the shelves. If instructed to return a toy to the shelf, he might respond by throwing it across the room. Michael would say he had to go to the bathroom. Once in the bathroom, he would engage in activities like filling the sink with water and letting it run all over the floor.

Michael's behavior at naptime was not surprising. Young children who have been sexually abused very often resist going to sleep or lying down to rest. Teachers in the program were understanding and loving. They were determined to find a humane solution for dealing with Michael's naptime problems.

Something needed to be done quickly since Michael was keeping an entire class of children awake. Teachers tried rubbing Michael's back. The room was darkened and soft music was played. They tried giving Michael quiet activities to do on his mat if he couldn't sleep. Activities included looking at books, playing with small toys, coloring and puzzles. All of the activities seemed to provide a way for Michael to make noise. Then teachers tried taking Michael for walks, thinking that walking might make Michael tired enough to rest.

Finally, a behavioral assessment was conducted. We noticed that the times that Michael seemed the calmest were when he was watching the classroom's parakeet or gerbil. He would stand at the cages for long periods of time to watch the classroom pets while other children played with toys. Michael was told that a new plan would be started during naptime. If he could stay quietly on his mat, the gerbil would be placed on a low table next to him. He was permitted to sit up to watch the gerbil and he was given a selection of quiet activities.

On the first day the gerbil was present during Michael's nap, he had no trouble staying quiet. The gerbil seemed to provide all the stimulation Michael needed. The teachers got together at the end of the day. While they were all thrilled with Michael's behavior in the presence of the gerbil, they all predicted it was a novelty effect and that within a week, Michael would be running around the room during nap. Having seen plenty of hyperactive children lose interest in small animals after a short time, I tended to agree with them. Happily, we were wrong. Michael had a history that resulted in him not wanting to be alone during naptime. He needed something to do that was mentally engaging. The gerbil provided the stimulation and companionship that Michael needed in order to have a naptime that was calm and restful.

PART III

Where You Can Volunteer With Your Pet

CHAPTER 8

Nursing Homes

VISITING A NURSING HOME

Nursing homes are the most commonly visited animal-assisted therapy settings. Many nursing home residents are depressed and lonely and your visit with your animal will provide people with companionship, love and something to look forward to.

CHARACTERISTICS OF PEOPLE IN NURSING HOMES

People go to live in nursing homes when they can no longer care for themselves independently. Many nursing home residents have health problems that require routine medical care. As a volunteer in a nursing home, you and your animal will be working with people who may have dementia, confusion, Alzheimer's disease, hearing problems, vision problems or blindness and speech problems. Nursing home residents may also have physical problems that result in decreased mobility and strength, and problems with walking and balance. Most nursing home residents are elderly, but there are some exceptions to this.

In nursing homes, animals can provide companionship and something to look forward to.
Courtesy of Ed Silverman, Jewish Home and Delta Society

WORKING WITH PEOPLE IN NURSING HOMES

As you volunteer in a nursing home or any other setting, always ask yourself the question, "Would I like to be treated this way?" In all types of facilities, always be aware of client confidentiality. Confidentiality means that what you see and hear in any facility stays there. It is not appropriate to talk about clients with people outside of the facility. You should not take photographs unless you have checked with the client and staff, and then an official photo release should be signed before you take a picture of any client. There are laws pertaining to confidentiality. Violations of confidentiality can result in legal action.

When you are working with older people, you should be patient and understanding. Remember that unless we have terminal illnesses or injuries, all of us will be elderly some day. You should be caring and responsible of all the people you meet as a volunteer, as well as genuine.

TALKING TO A PERSON IN A WHEELCHAIR

When you are visiting with a person who is in a wheelchair, remember to talk directly to the person, even if a staff person is present.

A friend of mine is a professor with the IQ of a genius. She raised three children as a single parent. Two became lawyers, the other is a biomedical engineer. It just so happens that my friend uses a wheelchair. Once when we were in a restaurant, a waitress said to a member of our party, "What would *she* like to eat?"

Remember that walkers, wheelchairs and canes are simply mobility aids. They have nothing to do with a person's mental functioning level. Adults who are in wheelchairs do not like to be talked to in babytalk or patted on the head.

It is not appropriate to sit or lean on a person's wheelchair. To make conversations easier, you can sit or kneel to put yourself at eye level with the person using the wheelchair. If a person in a wheelchair is moving slowly, don't simply start pushing the chair. You should always ask the person if he or she would like assistance before you push the chair.

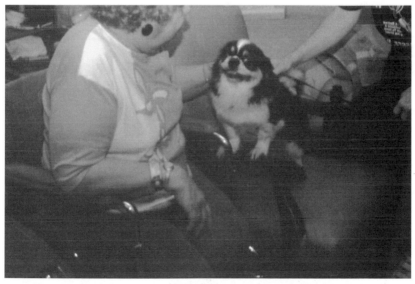

Smaller animals can be placed beside clients for visiting.
Courtesy of Cynda Crawford, PhD, DVM, and Patty

Larger therapy dogs can be positioned to stand beside wheel-chairs. If a person in a wheelchair does not wish to hold your smaller animal, the animal can be placed in a chair beside the wheelchair for the visit.

DEMENTIA, ALZHEIMER'S DISEASE AND CONFUSION

The techniques for working with people with dementia, Alzheimer's disease or general confusion are similar. Elderly people may be confused from time to time. When confusion is constant and severe, the person may have a condition such as dementia or Alzheimer's disease.

Dementia is a loss of mental abilities severe enough to interfere with normal social or everyday functioning. With dementia, memory, judgment, abstract thought and overall personality are changed. Memory impairment can range from difficulty with memory tasks, such as remembering the names of certain objects, to the inability to recognize family members. People with dementia may have a hard time coping with new situations.

In the advanced stages of dementia, clients may exhibit a lack of personal hygiene (unless they are cared for by others), foul language, irritability and lethargy. The best known cause of dementia is Alzheimer's disease, but strokes, concussions, neurological diseases and exposure to toxic substances (including legal and illegal drugs) can cause dementia.

Alzheimer's disease is an incurable degenerative disease of the brain. While many of us have only heard of Alzheimer's in recent years, this disease was first described in 1906 by Alois Alzheimer, a German neuropathologist. Alzheimer's disease causes progressive dementia, and the primary symptom is memory loss. Other Alzheimer's disease symptoms may include problems with language, abstract reasoning and visual–spatial abilities. Personality changes that are present with dementia occur in Alzheimer's disease. These personality changes may include apathy and agitation. In the advanced stages of Alzheimer's disease, clients may have psychiatric symptoms that include depression, delusions and hallucinations.

Alzheimer's disease is the most common cause of dementia in adults, and more than two million people over the age of 65 are affected by the disease. Doctors can diagnose Alzheimer's disease by using diagnostic procedures that show if dying neurons are present in the brain. The cause of Alzheimer's disease is not known. Risk factors include advanced age and genetic predisposition. To date, drugs to correct the effects of Alzheimer's disease do not exist, but new drugs are being developed and tested with the hopes that there will soon be a medication available that can relieve the symptoms of Alzheimer's disease.

TAKE PRECAUTIONS

When you volunteer with your pet in a setting where people have Alzheimer's disease, dementia or confusion, there are some things that you can do to maximize the effectiveness of your visit.
- Conversations should be in quiet areas.
- Approach the client and make sure that the client wants to see your pet.
- Before you start talking, make sure the client is looking at you. If the person is looking out into space, position yourself and your pet so you can be seen. You might gently touch the person on the arm or hand to make your presence known.
- Speak in a calm voice.
- Speak slowly so the person can understand you.
- If the person has problems understanding, use short, simple language.
- If the person is not responding to your questions or looking at your animal, ask permission, then very gently guide their hands to pet your animal. If you are going to touch a client you do not know well, a staff person should be present to observe the first interaction.
- Rather than use excessive language, bring props to your visit. These may include photos of you and your pet at home, a brochure from a place you visited or a seashell you found on the beach.
- If the client has memory problems, you can repeat concepts during the visit.

- If you ask questions, ask only one at a time and give the client adequate time to respond.
- Use plenty of reassurance to make the person feel safe.
- If the person does not wish to talk, you can tell a story about your animal.
- Observe clients closely to make sure they are not getting overly tired or bored with the visit. Watch for signs of withdrawal or restlessness.

CLIENTS WITH HEARING PROBLEMS

Many people who are elderly experience some loss of hearing. The following tips might help you when you are volunteering with clients who are hearing impaired.

- Visit with the client in a place that has no distracting background noise.
- Place yourself so the client can see your mouth and read your lips.
- Stand or sit at the client's eye level.
- Speak clearly.
- Do not speak too quickly or mumble.
- Be patient and calmly repeat your message if the client could not understand you.

CLIENTS WITH VISION PROBLEMS

- Do not touch a person who is blind without their permission (e.g., "May I guide your hand to show you where the dog is?").
- Be sure to introduce yourself at the beginning of the visit.
- You can describe things that are going on during the visit ("The bird can hear the music and he is rocking on his perch.").
- Don't forget to tell the client when you are leaving and when you will return.

THERAPY ACTIVITIES IN NURSING HOMES

In nursing home settings, there will be a wide range of client goals you and your animal can work on with direction from facility professionals.

Cognitive/knowledge
- Memory—talking about the past
- Remembering information about the therapy animal
- Remembering information about animals owned in the past
- Talking about animals, recalling information about breeds and their care
- Recalling information about animal-related movies or television shows

Gross Motor (big muscles—arms and legs)
- Ambulation (a common nursing plan treatment goal is ambulation, which is simply walking. Clients can take therapy animals for walks or they can walk from their rooms to a day room to visit a therapy animal)
- Throwing a ball for a therapy animal
- Swinging arm at a toy for a therapy animal
- Reaching to touch a therapy animal
- Bending from sitting to pet a therapy animal placed at feet

Fine Motor (hands)
- Petting the therapy animal
- Touching a specified body part (on the therapy animal)
- Tying a ribbon on a dog
- Buckling a collar
- Feeding a treat to the therapy animal (handler and facility permission)

Speech/communication
- Talking about the therapy animal
- Talking about animals owned in the past
- Telling others about animals owned in the past (socialization)

Daily Living
- Feeding the animal (if appropriate)
- Walking the animal
- Taking care of facility animals
- Making a purchase for facility animals

CASE STUDY: A THERAPY DOG OVERCOMES ANIMOSITY

For months my Border Collie, Laddie, and I had been visiting a particular nursing home. We had a caseload of clients that was assigned to us for each visit. After several months, we knew most of the clients in the facility. On some days, I visited without my dog in order to spend time with clients who didn't like animals. I got to know one woman, Mrs. Grandy, who was fearful and didn't want Laddie to come near her. I made it a point to spend time with Mrs. Grandy on my non-dog visits.

Mrs. Grandy was fearful and negative about everything. Asked if she'd like to go for a walk, she'd put a quiver in her voice and say, "I'm so afraid, I might fall." Trying to reason with her seemed to reinforce fearful verbal behavior. If I said I understood and I'd walk with someone else, I would no sooner be part way down the hall when Mrs. Grandy would nearly knock me down in her efforts to catch up and go on the walk.

Mrs. Grandy had negative verbal behavior most of the time. When I asked her to go with me to hear the children sing, she responded with, "No, I hate children." When I ignored the response and went without her, there she was, plopping herself down right beside me in the front row. When the singing was over,

I smiled and said, "Wasn't that great? We sure had fun singing." She would scowl at me and snap, "You were off-key."

I began to notice that no matter where I was in the facility when I visited with Laddie, Mrs. Grandy was somewhere nearby. One day, I said, "Mrs. Grandy, would you like to pet Laddie?" As always, she responded, "No, I'm afraid. I'm afraid he'll bite me." "Well," I said, "Laddie doesn't bite. He is very well trained. You will be amazed at what he can do. Would you like to sit there and watch some of his tricks?"

She squinted her eyes and would not give me the satisfaction of indicating she was interested in Laddie's tricks. I kept on going. "You see, this dog can do all kinds of things. If you were tired and didn't want to get your shoes, he could get them for you." By then, a crowd of clients had gathered for the show. I took off my shoe and threw it down the hall. Yawning, I said, "Laddie, I'm so tired. Please get my shoe," as I gave the hand signal for a retrieve. In a flash Laddie was sitting in front of me with the shoe. All of the clients were cheering and applauding. All except Mrs. Grandy. "How did you like it?" I asked. Mrs. Grandy tried her best to sound grouchy, but I'm sure I saw a smile. "I bet he can't do the other one," she said.

Mrs. Grandy, Laddie and I went on like this for weeks. Nurses were concerned because she never said anything positive to anyone. Clients avoided interacting with her. Professional staff had given up on trying to model good social skills. Valentine's Day arrived and a television crew came to the facility to film a segment on Laddie working with clients. I set up the room for the live filming and invited clients to participate who liked the dog.

The nurses were standing in the hall prepared to stop any clients who tried to wander into the filming area. The cameras were rolling and Laddie was doing great. All of a sudden, a client who was to be on film got up and left the filming area. That left an empty seat, and Mrs. Grandy slipped past the nurses and sat down. The television interviewer assumed she was there to say something positive and went over to her. "So what do you think of this dog?" he asked in his deep media voice. I knew at that moment that if she opened her mouth, my career in animal-assisted therapy was over. Mrs. Grandy got up. She walked right past the interviewer and over to the video camera. My heart was pounding; Mrs. Grandy hadn't had a positive thing to say since the day we met her. She put her face about twelve inches from the camera and in response to the interviewer repeating the question, "So what do you think of this dog?" she replied on live television, "He's pretty damn good."

Mrs. Grandy seemed negative. Somehow, her verbal behavior had been shaped to be negative. But when all was said and done, every time I volunteered at the facility with Laddie, Mrs. Grandy tracked us down. Despite the words she was saying, the dog was a reinforcing event and was something she looked forward to.

CHAPTER 9

Developmental Disabilities Facilities

If you decide to volunteer in a developmental disabilities setting, the most common disabilities you will see include mental retardation, cerebral palsy and autism. Here is a description of each so you know what to look for and expect.

MENTAL RETARDATION

Mental retardation is characterized by "significantly subaverage general intellectual functioning." In the formal definition, to be "mentally retarded" there must also be impairments in adaptive behavior and onset of the condition during the childhood years.

Subaverage general intellectual functioning relates to IQ scores, and to be classified as mentally retarded, an individual's IQ needs to be below 70. A normal IQ score is 100.

Impairments in adaptive behavior mean that the person also lacks skills in daily living activities such as grooming or following directions. The requirement that retardation should have the childhood years as the time of onset is to distinguish the condition from head injury or similar categories, where a person may lose skills and intellectual abilities as an adult.

Mental retardation affects two to three percent of the population. The majority of people with retardation are mildly retarded and can function with minimal support in the community. More males than females are mentally retarded. Mentally retarded people may have other conditions accompanying their retardation which can include cerebral palsy and mental disorders such as schizophrenia.

As a volunteer, you could work in school programs, day treatment or residential settings for individuals with retardation. Individuals with mental retardation will learn slowly, and volunteers in these settings should be patient people. There are many exciting goals and objectives you and your pet can work on in settings for people who are mentally retarded, so don't be discouraged.

CEREBRAL PALSY

Cerebral palsy is a condition in which brain damage either before or during birth causes some degree of paralysis. The most common cause of cerebral palsy is a traumatic injury at birth. Birth injuries can be caused when forceps are used and the head is compressed, when the umbilical cord strangles the infant or when the infant is deprived of oxygen.

Some infections such as mumps, measles and toxoplasmosis may increase the risk of cerebral palsy. Excessive exposure to toxic chemicals, including alcohol, can increase the risks of cerebral palsy. The effects of cerebral palsy vary greatly. Individuals may have no use of their arms or legs or any of the muscles that aid in speech, or they may only have a minor problem, such as a slight limp.

Since so many people with cerebral palsy have physical problems, many of the treatment goals for these clients will be of a physical nature. As a volunteer, you and your pet can work on skills as advanced as walking, or as basic as opening a hand to prevent muscles from becoming further contracted.

Therapy animals can be used to teach advanced or basic skills.

AUTISM

Autism is a disability that primarily affects an individual's language and social abilities. In most cases, autism is diagnosed in the first three years of life. Autistic children are usually normal in their appearance, and their most noticeable deficit is usually in the area of communication. For every 10,000 births there are four to five autistic children. Three times as many boys are autistic as girls. Over the past few decades, theories about the causes of autism have changed. It was once believed that autism was related to a child's poor relationship (lack of bonding) with the mother, or that there had been some emotional trauma. It is currently believed that autism has a biological basis.

The majority of people who have been diagnosed as autistic are also classified as mentally retarded. Autism comes from the Greek word *autos* meaning "self," and most autistic people seem to be unattached to the world around them. They may appear aloof and unresponsive to normal social interactions. Many autistic individuals engage in self-stimulatory behaviors such as hand flapping, rocking and spinning toys or small objects. Some autistic individuals will have unusual habits (like collecting objects of a certain shape or color) and they may avoid eye contact.

As an animal-assisted therapy volunteer in settings for people with autism, you might find that children will stop engaging in self-stimulatory behaviors in the presence of your pet. If you work closely with professional staff, you will be able to use your pet to teach goals that include following directions, increasing attention span, basic language and selected functional tasks.

PEOPLE WITH DEVELOPMENTAL DISABILITIES AND THE COMMUNITY

No matter what the developmental disability, there is a growing trend in this country toward a concept called "inclusion." Inclusion means that people with disabilities should be included in the activities of people with no disabilities. If we teach a child with mental retardation to walk a dog at the special day school the child attends, the program is not complete until that child has learned to walk the dog in the community. If we teach an adult with mental retardation to do some basic obedience training with a dog, the inclusion model would state that the program is not complete until the client has some level of participation in a community obedience class. As a volunteer in a developmental disabilities setting, you may be able to help with inclusion activities.

SKILLS YOU CAN TEACH IN DD SETTINGS

Skills you can teach using animal-assisted therapy in developmental disabilities settings include:

Cognitive/knowledge
• Recalling information about animals, breeds
• Remembering/naming the animal and volunteer
• Telling how a particular therapy animal should be cared for

Gross Motor (big muscles—arms and legs)

- Walking with a dog or cat
- Throwing a ball for a dog
- Running to get a ball for a dog
- Hitting at a toy suspended from a string for a cat
- Holding arm out to take a bird
- Passing a basket or cage of a small animal to another person
- Moving wheelchair to get to animal
- Walking to get to a therapy animal

Fine Motor (hands)

- Brushing or combing the therapy animal
- Cleaning a cage or pen (may also be gross motor if shoveling or raking is involved)
- Fastening a leash or collar
- Getting a treat from a box or package
- Feeding a treat to the therapy animal (with handler's permission). If there is any concern the client does not have the fine motor control to release the treat, treats can be offered in a clothespin, on the end of a long wooden spoon or in a plastic bowl held by the client
- Opening fingers (if hands are contracted) to pet the therapy animal

Speech/Communication

- Answering questions about the therapy animal
- Telling another person about the therapy animal
- Telling about a past history with pets
- Saying the animal's name
- Imitating an animal sound
- Giving a hand signal to a therapy animal
- Giving a verbal command to a therapy animal
- Talking to the animal

Daily Living
• Responsibility
• Showing up at an appointed time to care for an animal
• Completing animal care tasks (feeding, cleaning pen)

Vocational
• Performing vocational animal-related tasks (e.g., cleaning stalls)
• Reporting the animal's status to a designated staff person
• Learning basic dog obedience with the therapy dog

ADVANTAGES AND DISADVANTAGES OF VOLUNTEERING IN A DEVELOPMENTAL DISABILITIES SETTING

Volunteering in a developmental disabilities setting can be an extremely enriching experience. You will be thrilled when you and your pet have been able to teach a developmentally disabled individual how to do something for the first time. In many settings, the staff will welcome you as a member of the treatment team, and your pet will get a lot of attention from clients and staff.

Many of these settings are chronically short-staffed. That means that people scramble to get the basic care of the clients completed. Volunteers may not be given much help or guidance and staff might be reluctant to spend time helping you. Some of the clients will have behavior problems, and volunteers need to have the proper training and "temperament" for dealing with this. Sometimes clients in developmental disabilities facilities fight and argue over therapy animals ("It's my dog," "No, it's mine!") and you will need to be prepared to handle such situations.

CASE STUDY: USING A THERAPY DOG WITH AUTISTIC CHILDREN

Phobias are fears that are so extreme they affect a person's ability to function in a normal manner. A phobia is a clinical disorder that should be treated by a qualified professional. The following

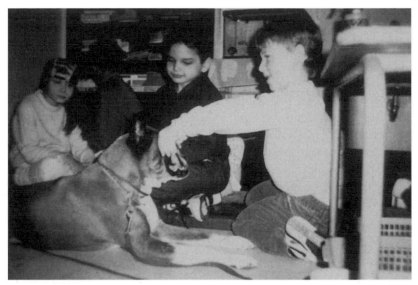

Trained therapy dogs can be used in treating dog phobia.
Courtesy of Ann Lettis and Will

case describes the treatment of two autistic children who were dog phobic. A volunteer and her therapy dog worked in conjunction with two professionals to implement the treatment plan.

Being dog phobic makes life difficult for the average person. When we are dealing with people who are autistic or mentally retarded, dog phobia can be a serious problem, manifesting itself in dangerous behaviors such as running into traffic when dogs are approaching on the sidewalk.

Mary Jane Gill, PhD, was the psychologist at the program for children with autism at the Bayley Seton Hospital in Staten Island, New York. Several of the children in the program were dog phobic. These students made it impossible for teachers to take the class for walks in the community. When a dog came to visit, the excessive reactions of the phobic children caused other children to become afraid of animals.

James was a thirteen-year-old autistic boy who functioned in the severe range of mental retardation. He could communicate using a combination of verbal speech and sign language. He reacted to dogs with extreme fear. On several occasions, when a dog was approaching on the sidewalk, he would run away in fright with no awareness of potential dangers such as traffic. When he was pursued, he would become violently aggressive. When he was at home, his family had stopped taking him out of his own yard because he became uncontrollable if he saw a dog.

Ann Lettis and her Boxer, Will, were volunteering at Bayley Seton. Lettis became aware of James and called me to ask for advice. I had worked with dog phobic children before and was able to consult with Dr. Gill, the psychologist, on implementing a program. In the beginning of the therapy, James's phobia was so severe he showed fear reactions to stuffed dogs and pictures of dogs. After several sessions, he tolerated these stimuli and the real dog, Will, was introduced. From the first time the dog was present until James was comfortable enough to pet Will, there were twelve treatment sessions, each lasting twenty minutes.

The first session began with the dog twenty feet away from James. Over time, the dog was moved closer. James had a chair in the doorway of the room and was permitted to leave at any time he became uncomfortable. The treatment plan was a thirteen-step program that involved systematically bringing the dog closer to James. This is how it progressed:

1. Child enters room with dog twenty feet away.
2. Child sits in chair with dog twenty feet away.
3. Child stays in room for five minutes with dog twenty feet away.
4. Child stays in room with dog fifteen feet away.
5. Child stays in room with dog twelve feet away.
6. Child stays in room for ten minutes with dog ten feet away.
7. Child stays in room with dog eight feet away.
8. Child stays in room with dog six feet away.
9. Child stays in room for fifteen minutes with dog five feet away.
10. Child stays in room for twenty minutes with dog four feet away.
11. Child stays in room for twenty minutes with dog three feet away.

12. Child holds end of leash.
13. Child pets dog.

Eventually, other dogs were added to the treatment program to ensure that the results would generalize to other dogs. James and his friends also were taught skills about interacting with dogs (like you should always ask if you may pet someone's dog). The final step of the program came when James was able to once again go on outings with his family and enjoy this world that we share with dogs.

This work has been replicated with several other dog phobic children. In addition to providing effective treatment for the children involved, this case had some interesting features. Ann Lettis was a volunteer who was connected with a national network. Because of that, when she had a problem, she was instantly able to pick up the phone and get some technical assistance. Mary Jane Gill was not trained in animal-assisted therapy and was willing to use information provided by another professional via phone consultations. The use of a well-trained therapy dog with these dog phobic children ensured that the children would be treated in the presence of an animal that was reliable, predictable and under control at all times. If Will was told to stay, the only movement we saw was the blinking of his eyes. He made no unpredictable movements that would scare children and reduce treatment progress. This was a situation where a volunteer and her dog were able to demonstrate (under the direction of a professional) that the standard procedures used to treat phobias can be greatly enhanced when trained, certified therapy dogs are used in the treatment.

CASE STUDY: ASSISTING AN ADULT WITH MILD MENTAL RETARDATION

Perry was a twenty-seven-year-old man who functioned in the mild range of mental retardation (his IQ was 65). He could dress and bathe himself and he had some basic cooking skills. He could make an "X" on paper as a signature and he had good social skills. Perry was living in a residential sixty-four-bed facility and it was hoped that he could learn some additional skills and move to a group home. The group home that was under consideration was in a nice neighborhood. Eight clients lived in the group home and there were staff members present at all times to supervise activities.

To be admitted to the group home, clients had to work at some job, even if the job was at a staff-supervised (sheltered) workshop. To get a sheltered work placement (or any job), Perry needed to demonstrate good work behaviors. In particular, he needed to show up on time, start his job (usually an assembly task), stay on task and finish the work. Staying on task meant that he worked at his work station until it was time for an official break or lunch.

To prepare Perry for sheltered employment, the residential facility had developed a schedule of "classes" throughout the day where Perry would learn work tasks. And that's where the trouble began. Perry didn't like going to work, but he wanted to move to the group home. "Getting his own place," he called it. Perry would show up late for the classes, even though he could tell time. When he finally got to class, he would stay a short time and leave to walk about the facility and visit with secretaries and administrative staff. We also noticed that he enjoyed visiting with the resident Beagle far more than he enjoyed going to class.

I decided that Perry needed to learn that class could be a reinforcing place. We dispensed with the original curriculum and told Perry he was going to learn to care for the dog. It took him nearly a month to complete task analysis programs on filling food and water pans and taking the food to the dog, but he did it. He started showing up for class early waiting to learn the dog care skills. We then started systematically building a chain of behavior. Perry was required to complete one regular assembly task, then he could work on the dog skills and see the dog. We continued adding tasks until, eventually, Perry worked the entire morning on sheltered work activities and took the dog for a walk during his lunch break.

Perry eventually moved to a group home, and he now works all day at a sheltered workshop. As a part of inclusion, he is involved in dog-related activities in the community. He arranged for me to give a presentation on dog training at an Association of Retarded

Citizens meeting. When the humane society has free flea bathing on weekends, Perry is there volunteering his time. He's always soaked, he's always smiling and he always tells me how great he's doing at his job.

CASE STUDY: ASSISTING A CHILD WITH PROFOUND MENTAL RETARDATION AND CEREBRAL PALSY

Billy was a twelve-year-old boy who lived in a residential facility. He had cerebral palsy that affected both his arms and legs. At twelve, Billy weighed only forty pounds. He did not walk or talk and was not toilet-trained. Billy's hands were fixed in contracted positions. Both wrists bent forward as far as possible, and Billy would not straighten his hands. From moisture and pressure, the tissue on the insides of Billy's wrists was starting to break down and the problem was seen by facility staff as a medical priority.

The occupational therapist (OT) completed an evaluation and decided that Billy needed regular range-of-motion exercises. Range-of-motion involves body parts being gently exercised by a trained person. The OT trained the staff and Billy was to have range-of-motion exercises every day. Billy did not like the exercises. Billy screamed during the sessions, resisting having some one gently try to open his hands even the slightest bit, and the staff disliked performing the therapy.

I was called in to find a reinforcer that could be provided if Billy complied with the routine. Billy did not respond to any traditional reinforcers (food, drink, vibration, music, touch or toys). One day, I saw a staff member pushing him in his wheelchair through the courtyard. He had a huge smile on his face and he was watching the resident dog. We'd found a reinforcer.

"Billy," I said, "Here's the dog. Do you want to feed her a dog biscuit?" I held up a box of dog biscuits. His smile lit up the room. "OK, you have to do your exercises so you can get a biscuit." I manipulated each wrist for a few seconds only and said, "Good, you did your exercises. Let's get a biscuit for the dog." With hand-over-hand guidance, I moved Billy's hands through the motions of getting a dog biscuit from the box. The dog took the treat, licked Billy and he squealed with delight.

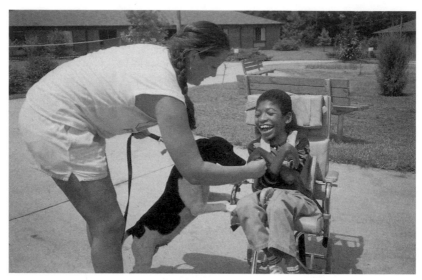

Children with severe disabilities can benefit from interactions with therapy animals.

We continued to increase the length of time that each hand was exercised before Billy got to get a biscuit from the box and give it to the dog.

There were some dramatic measurable gains in Billy's case. Occupational and physical therapists can measure how far a joint can move using a tool called a goniometer. A goniometer looks like some equipment from a high school geometry class. At the first quarterly review of Billy's progress, the OT gave her report. Billy was opening both wrists to forty-five degrees and there was no more tissue breakdown.

In the cases of Billy and Perry, we were using a residential dog in the therapy program. After Billy made progress on his OT goal, we started using the dog as a reinforcer in a program designed to teach Billy to communicate using a picture language board. (With language boards, nonverbal clients look at pictures to indicate needs.) Billy was making progress, but unfortunately the program ended due to staff shortages. In times of funding problems or staff shortages, it is hard to justify having extra people present in therapy to serve as dog handlers. If a volunteer had been available (with or without a pet), Billy's program could have continued.

CHAPTER 10

Schools

The uses of animal-assisted therapy in schools are endless. In school settings, animals can be used to work on a wide range of skills and activities, depending on the needs and ages of the students. Some classrooms have pets. Small animals such as guinea pigs, hamsters, birds and fish are most common in preschool through elementary school classrooms. In some classrooms, a staff person has been permitted to bring a dog or cat to work each day so the class has a mascot animal.

Some schools welcome volunteers and their pets as a part of the educational program. Volunteers can teach humane education, or they can work with teachers on specific goals and objectives for students. In cases where children have problems, animal-assisted therapy might be used to incorporate animals into counseling programs. Volunteers can work with the same class on an ongoing basis or can go to different classes or school assemblies to give a one-time lecture or demonstration.

Some volunteers in school settings work with the humane society or wildlife rehabilitation agencies to provide educational programs. A different school or class can be visited each time, or volunteers can work primarily with one school or classroom.

As an animal-assisted therapy volunteer in schools, you can choose to work with special-needs children or with regular education students.

DEVELOPING A PROGRAM

There are excellent materials available for working with children in schools. The American Humane Association and the American Kennel Club have free materials available about bringing dogs into school programs. Contact these organizations for information. You can write to The American Humane Association at 9725 East Hampden Ave., Denver, CO 80321. Contact the American Kennel Club at 51 Madison Ave., New York, NY 10010; attn.: Public Education Department.

The curriculum of the Pet Education Partnership (PEP) provides an excellent guide for teaching children an appreciation of animals. The Pet Education Partnership is a program of the People-Pet-Partnership. The PEP manual, "Learning and Living Together: Building the Human Animal Bond," includes sections on starting a pet education program, training volunteers and instructors, and teaching methods. More than half of the manual is lesson plans for preschool through sixth grade. For preschool and Grade 1, the lesson is "Getting Acquainted with Pets." Second grade students learn about understanding the needs of pets in a lesson called, "Little Critters as Pets." In third grade, students are introduced to the physical and behavioral traits of animals in a lesson called, "Cats as Pets." Fourth graders learn to begin making decisions about which pet would be right for them in a "Dogs as Pets" lesson. To begin to teach appreciation for wild animals, the lesson "Wild Animals Are Not Pets" is introduced in fifth grade. The final lesson, "The Living Bond," teaches students how animals can help us in tasks such as therapy, search and rescue and police work.

SETTING GOALS FOR SCHOOL ATTENDEES

There are hundreds of goals that can be worked on when you volunteer with your pet in schools. You can teach all kinds of

Interacting with an animal can boost a child's self-esteem.
Courtesy of Delta Society, Linda Kaufman and Zuma

cognitive (knowledge) skills and you can work on motor (physical) skills. You can use the animal in humane education programs and you can teach about animal care and training. Because the list of skills is so long since the needs of students vary based on age, the three scenarios below describe the types of animal-assisted therapy activities that can be done in different school settings. In addition to the activities below, students can get involved in learning about and caring for classroom pets. Interacting with an animal can boost the self-esteem of many children.

CASE STUDIES: ASSISTING IN PRESCHOOL, MIDDLE SCHOOL AND COLLEGE

PRESCHOOL

I was called to bring my Border Collie, Laddie, to Mrs. Thomas's pre-kindergarten class. Her class was located at a public school and the program was an "early intervention" program. Children had been placed in the program because they were developmentally delayed or because they had speech or language problems. Mrs. Thomas was a veteran teacher who was extremely competent. She knew me from my work as an early childhood consultant, but when she asked about me visiting with the dog, she made it clear she wanted to run the activity. That was fine with me. I decided to "play it straight" and go to her class in the role of a naive volunteer.

I could have done a good job if Mrs. Thomas had let me be in charge of the visit, but Mrs. Thomas did a *great* job. The difference was that she knew each of the children well and she constantly thought about their individual needs and goals. When I came in the first time, she had the children sitting in a circle. She was just finishing a short lesson on how we should interact with dogs. "Should we yell and scare the dog?" "NOOOO!" sixteen eager voices shouted. "If you're afraid of the dog, should you run and scream?" "NOOO!" was once again the response. "That's right," she said. "This will be a nice dog. We don't want to scare him. He will be on a leash, and we will ask each of you if you want to get close to him." Thinking of all the times I entered a classroom with a dog only to be met by hysterical, screaming children, I was very grateful for Mrs. Thomas's understanding of what behaviorists call antecedent (before an event) control.

Mrs. Thomas called the children one or two at a time to come up and pet Laddie. She was close by to work with each child and the dog. Robert had a really hard time learning colors, but by the time we left on the first visit, he knew black and white because of Laddie's fur coat. Jessie just couldn't get it straight about body parts. Nose was easy, mouth and eyes were hard to remember. In less than five minutes, she learned to point to Laddie's mouth and eyes, and then her own.

On some days, Janie would look around the immediate area during an activity and begin to cry. Mrs. Thomas figured out she was crying because she did not see an adult nearby and she thought she had been left. She was trying to teach her to carefully visually scan the whole classroom. For Janie, Laddie needed to move around the room. I got his toy and had one child go and hide it in the classroom as Laddie and I hid. Laddie was then told to "find it," which he did by using his keen sense of smell. The children were delighted, and with Mrs. Thomas sitting at her side and prompting her to watch, Janie visually tracked the dog through the entire activity.

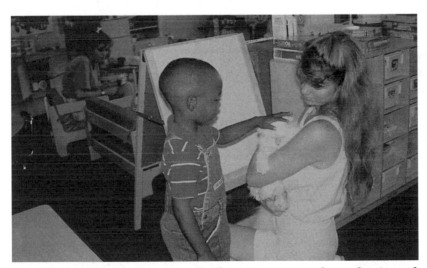

Animals can be used in preschool settings to teach academic and social concepts.
Courtesy of Delight Hicks

Melanie was afraid of dogs, but by the end of the first visit, she was willing to touch Laddie's hind quarters if he laid down and Mrs. Thomas held his head. Mrs. Thomas was a person Melanie knew and trusted.

Mrs. Thomas ended our first visit by talking to the children about kindness, how we care for pets and what they need to live. Before that visit, I thought that only a skilled animal-assisted therapist could engineer a visit of such high quality. Mrs. Thomas was a wonderful teacher, and with a volunteer and dog present, she was able to use the dog to teach a wide range of skills to the children. I sure learned a lot at preschool that day.

Middle School

I was called to a middle school to give a demonstration on dog training. Teenagers are not really a preferred population for me. I like working with very young children, older people, people with disabilities and, well, just about anybody but teenagers. But Mrs. Klein begged me to come in and get the students in her science class fired up so that they all joined the Animal Club at school. I talked to the class about the Canine Good Citizen Test and did a demonstration of basic good manners for dogs. Then I showed them some Utility (advanced) obedience exercises and explained that with hard work and consistency, their dogs could learn to do these behaviors.

I didn't have any plans on that day to do humane education. I was there to talk about training. When it was time for questions and answers, most of the students wanted a solution to a problem they had with their own pet. "My dog digs out of the yard," "Our cat keeps on marking the corner of my mom's bedspread," and "My hamster runs around in his cage and keeps me awake at night," were examples.

One boy raised his hand and gave me an intense, nervous look. I was wondering what kind of problem his pet would have. "Is it true most of the animals in shelters are killed?" was his question. I wasn't expecting the question and hesitated just a moment before answering. Before I responded, the students were yelling at him, "No, that's not true," "Geez, Chris, you're so stupid."

The lesson then changed to a humane-education lesson. "I'm sorry to tell you all this is true." There was dead silence in the room. I gave them all of the ugly statistics (depending on what statistics you look at, an estimated fourteen million animals are euthanized each year in shelters) and told them that on the average, only one animal in ten will be adopted. Chris had tears in his eyes. It turned out that his dog, Princess, was chained in the back yard. Unspayed, she had just produced a litter of six cute puppies. Chris had given them all names. Then his mom announced that they would all be taken to the shelter where the shelter "would find them all good homes." Whether she herself was unaware of the reality or was simply trying to protect her son, I don't know. But I was very angry with her.

I followed up with Mrs. Klein and sent some humane education materials to the class a few days after my visit. Weeks later, she sent me a thank-you note for coming to the class and told me that Chris and his friends had made the puppies a project. They found homes for all but one, which Chris was going to keep. Chris told Mrs. Klein that Princess was getting "fixed." Well, I guess some teenagers are OK.

COLLEGE

Dr. Jon Bailey is a psychology professor at Florida State University. He teaches behavioral courses to undergraduates and graduate students. Every semester he goes into the introductory psychology classes to give a lecture about applied behavior analysis. A part of the lecture includes talking about operant conditioning. Bailey quickly figured out that showing behavior was a lot better than talking about it. He started borrowing my dog, Laddie, for demos in the classes.

At first, he talked about operant conditioning and principles like shaping, fading and chaining. Shaping, fading and chaining are operant procedures that apply to any kind of learner, whether that learner be an animal or human. Shaping involves breaking the task into smaller units and reinforcing closer approximations to a behavior. Shaping might be used to teach a dog who is fearful of a wheelchair to gradually get closer and have contact with a client in the chair.

In training, fading usually refers to the gradual fading of assistance or cues. In teaching a dog to go over a jump, many trainers begin by running over the jump with the dog. The assistance and cues are faded as the trainer simply walks to the jump and cues the dog, and eventually sends the dog over the jump with no help.

Chaining is the tying together of individual skills that have been taught in order to make a complete sequence. In the therapy setting, behaviors involving holding and fetching can be chained to result in a dog getting an object and taking it to a client.

Laddie would demonstrate and the students were asked how they would teach a particular behavior. At the end of the sessions, Bailey showed students how obedience behaviors could be used in a functional setting. He gave a demonstration of therapy dog tasks. Then the lesson had two parts, operant conditioning and animal-assisted therapy.

Animal-assisted therapy is making its way to university classrooms, like this one, where the dog is given a hand signal to "down."

In one class, students started asking questions about the behavior problems of their own pets. Bailey was shocked. With as much academic behavioral education as these students had had, they knew very little about how to care for or train the animals they owned. One young man with two Rottweilers wanted to teach them to fight over a toy. When Bailey asked him why in the world he would do such a thing, he said, "I want them to be competitive." The lecture format then took another turn. Information on the proper care of animals was added. Students were given information on the Canine Good Citizen Test and told that as future psychologists, it is irresponsible not to teach their dogs basic good manners.

The final addition to the lecture was made when Bailey learned that the numbers of animals surrendered at the animal shelter greatly increase just as college ends for the summer. Before leaving town to go home, students turn in their apartment keys *and* their pets. Humane education and responsible ownership became a final part of the curriculum.

It's one thing when uneducated people are not responsible owners. When college students with above average IQs, training in behavioral procedures and a commitment to becoming psychologists are not responsible owners, it is very disturbing.

Hopefully, in the future, more college courses will include information on the human–animal bond, animal-assisted therapy and what it means to be a responsible citizen and pet owner. Only then will universities have adequately prepared students to go out into the world.

If you want to volunteer with your pet in a school, you can work with people of all ages, ranging from preschool to college. At every age level, you can work with educators to make a difference.

CHAPTER 11

Hospitals

A TIME-HONORED TRADITION

One of the first uses of animal-assisted therapy in hospital settings occurred during World War I. American Red Cross nurses brought dogs to the Armed Forces Convalescent Center to be companions for servicemen who were patients at the center. Since that time, animals have been used in hospital settings to help patients forget about their illnesses or pain. If you choose to volunteer with your animal in a hospital setting, you will be involved in a relatively new application of animal-assisted therapy.

DOCUMENTED HEALTH BENEFITS

Most of the animal-assisted therapy results in hospital settings have been documented in the form of anecdotal stories. More data is needed in this area. However, there are some studies that show there are some clear medical benefits to having animals present in the health-care setting. In an article in *Nursing Research* magazine (M. Baun, 1984) it was reported that blood pressure, heart rate and respiration were all reduced when subjects greeted a dog, especially if a bond had been formed with the animal.

Research in medical settings has also shown patients are more sociable and experience less loneliness and depression when animals are present.

MODEL PROGRAMS

There are a number of model animal-assisted therapy programs in hospital settings. Good Samaritan Hospital in Phoenix, Arizona, has had an animal-assisted therapy program in place for several years. The program began with a single volunteer/dog team in 1991, and by 1994, there were twelve certified therapy dogs and handlers volunteering in several hospitals. In addition to regular therapy animal screening, all of the dogs were approved by the Arizona Department of Health. Services, medical staffs at each hospital and administrators of each hospital. With a written request from a patient's doctor, dogs can visit critical-care units.

One Good Samaritan cardiovascular surgeon routinely requests animal visits for his patients. Robin Tenny, the program coordinator for the program, described the therapeutic benefits of the therapy dogs, "Dogs make such able therapists because they are people oriented. They are irresistible to many people and their visits help patients forget, for a short time, the seriousness of their illness."

Major Lynn Anderson, DVM, MSW, of the U.S. Army Veterinary Corps, introduced animals to military medical treatment facilities. Anderson was appointed by the U.S. Army Surgeon General as the first military consultant on the human–animal bond.

At Columbia Hospital, in Milwaukee, Wisconsin, the Pet Companionship Program provides animal-assisted therapy visits to any patient in the hospital, on any unit. Jacquelyn McCurdy, RN, BSN, screens both animals and patients for the program. It is important that patients are not immuno-suppressed or post-surgical with draining wounds. In cases where patients share a room, the roommates must give permission for animal visits.

At the Denver Children's Hospital, dogs from the Prescription Pet Program visit select units to cheer up children who are sick or have cancer. Because there is concern about the dogs carrying "germs" or causing allergic reactions (via hair and dander), visiting dogs wear smocks that cover a majority of their back and sides. The program started in 1985 when Fran Bechtel noticed her paralyzed son's response to the family dog after months of being in the hospital. In the Denver program, physician and parental consent are required for visits. Nurses are present during the visits to assist and supervise volunteers.

In the San Francisco area, the Furry Friends Foundation was formed after Judy Kell's daughter was in the hospital and Kell realized the benefits animals could provide in a medical setting. The Furry Friends Foundation takes visiting animals to children's hospitals and specialized treatment homes. Some of the volunteers provide services through the recreation department at Stanford Children's Hospital. Animals used in the program include dogs, cats, rabbits, goats, sheep, birds, llamas and snakes.

ADVANTAGES AND DISADVANTAGES OF ANIMAL-ASSISTED THERAPY IN HOSPITALS

Animal visits in hospitals can take a patient's mind off of his or her problems and illness. Animals can be used to reduce pain, lower blood pressure or make a patient feel calmer. In general, hospitals are places where very few positive things happen to a patient; animals can be something to look forward to. Animals can motivate patients to improve in specific areas, such as fine-motor mobility.

Perhaps the most difficult animal-assisted therapy settings to gain access to are hospitals. In many medical settings, there is worry about zoonoses—diseases that can be transferred from animals to humans or humans to animals. Examples include psittacosis (an infection people can get from inhaling the secretions of an infected bird), toxoplasmosis (people can get this from handling cat litter boxes) and cat scratch fever.

Volunteers who want to work in hospitals should be prepared to spend more time preparing the animal for the visit than in the actual visits with patients. In other settings, it is acceptable to brush or comb dogs before visits. In hospitals, most programs require animals to be bathed before each visit. Patient allergies to animals are also of concern in medical settings, so all patients

Animals can motivate patients to improve in specific capacities, such as fine-motor skills. This man uses his hands to hold the cat and wave a toy. He is also smiling and watching.
Courtesy of Pat Gonser, PhD, RN, and Surefire

should be screened by medical staff before receiving animal-assisted therapy.

SPECIFIC BENEFITS OF THE THERAPY

The physical goals that animal-assisted therapy can address in a hospital setting are many. They include:

Physiological
- Lowering blood pressure
- Decreasing pulse
- Lowering stress level (petting animal, watching fish)
- Feeling less pain when animal is present

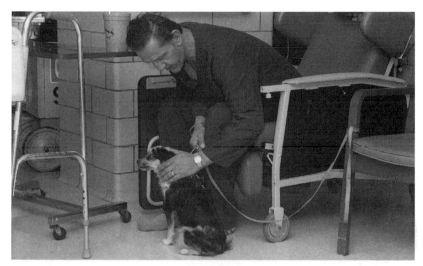

In hospitals, animals are used to improve trunk mobility and gross-motor movement. This man bends, pets the dog and holds the leash.
Courtesy Pat Gonser, PhD, RN, and Serenity

Sensory
- Visually tracking animal
- Tactile (touch)—feeling animal's fur

Motor Skills
- Reaching for animal (to one side or in front of body)
- Turning head to see animal
- Bending body at waist (trunk flexibility)
- Exercising hands by petting or brushing animal
- Exercising by walking animal (could be a vital part of treatment after surgery)

Speech/communication
- Imitating animal sound
- Saying animal's name (basic behaviors for a person with a stroke, etc.)

• Telling a family member about the animal (depressed person or child)

CASE STUDY: ANIMAL-ASSISTED THERAPY IN A MEDICAL SETTING

Pat Gonser, PhD, RN, is the executive director of Pets & People: Companions in Therapy and Service, based in Meridian, Mississippi. She is an expert in using animals in hospital settings to meet nursing treatment plan goals. Gonser has developed a comprehensive package of Nursing Treatment Care Plans for animal-assisted therapy in medical settings. This is a sample of one of her programs. She defines as precisely as she can the physical problems and the procedures to alleviate them.

Problems: Patient has problems with mobility and impaired physical movement. (Patients who cannot move can get pneumonia and bed sores. Breathing exercises and changing positions can help keep the lungs clear. Moving the body and changing positions can prevent bed sores.)

Type of Immobility: Client is confined to bed or reclining-type chair.

Goals:
1. Turn from side to side.
2. Take at least ten deep breaths.
3. No development of pressure areas.
4. Move upper body at least three times per day.

Intervention:
1. Place therapy animal at bedside in patient's line of vision. Verbally encourage patient to turn and reach for the animal. Move animal to opposite side of bed and repeat activity.
2. Place animal close to patient, facing away. Ask patient to breathe deeply and blow toward animal enough to part the coat.

3. Place small (lap) therapy animal on the patient's chest or abdomen. Encourage the patient to lift head off pillow to look at animal. Have patient reach to pet animal. Have patient hold trapeze, if available, and lift self off bed surface.

As can be seen from Gonser's plan, some of the procedures used in a medical setting might be technical and involve medical goals. Volunteers should only work on these goals under the direction of a qualified medical professional. The professional (a nurse, for example) can write the treatment plan, with the volunteer providing the animal and animal handling.

As of 1995, hospitals in the city in which I live (Tallahassee, Florida) did not allow visiting animals. This included both animal-assisted therapy volunteer/animal teams and the pets of patients. When a much-loved and well-respected dog trainer, Faye Simpson, was in our local hospital dying of cancer, she was unable to have the one thing that would have made her feel better—the chance to say good-bye to her dogs. We should all be grateful for the medical professionals in this country who have been progressive and open-minded enough to recognize that the therapeutic benefits of animals far outweigh the risks.

If you choose to volunteer with your pet in a hospital, you will be involved in improving the quality of life for hospitalized patients.

CHAPTER 12

Hospices and AIDS Settings

Opportunities do exist for volunteering in hospices and AIDS settings. In both situations, as a volunteer, you will need the ability to handle the eventual loss of your clients. While this may be difficult, there are great rewards in knowing that you and your pet were able to give people something to look forward to and to make their days brighter.

HOSPICES

Hospices are programs that provide an alternative to being in the hospital. The main goals of hospice programs are not to cure illnesses, but to ease the pain of terminally ill people and permit them to have natural deaths, free from obtrusive medical intervention.

The hospice movement is relatively new. The first hospice was founded in London in 1967. Since then, hospices have started in the United States as a means of providing patients with health care at home. In 1983, Medicare began covering costs for hospice care, and, as of 1995, there were nearly 3,000 hospice programs in the United States.

Hospice treatment is far less expensive than hospital treatment both for families and insurance companies that are providing medical coverage. Hospice treatment gives individuals the option of dying at home in the presence of familiar people, pets and possessions. For the most part, with hospice treatment, patients are not subjected to unnecessary, frequent medical interventions. Compared with many traditional medical settings, hospice programs give patients a chance to die with dignity.

Unfortunately, many hospice programs are overloaded with patients and they have staff shortages. Nurses and nurse assistants may cover multiple counties or geographical areas and have heavy caseloads. This means that a patient might only be seen every other day, or for a few minutes each day. If there is a medical emergency, qualified help is not right down the hall as it would be in a hospital. At the point at which hospice care is need, much of the patient's routine care is provided by a family member. Family members who are caretakers may experience exhaustion and mental health problems of their own before a patient's long illness is over.

AIDS PROGRAMS

AIDS, Acquired Immunodeficiency Syndrome, is a recently recognized disease. The first AIDS cases in this country were reported in 1981. In 1995, there were over 225,000 AIDS deaths in this country and an estimated one million Americans had been infected with the HIV virus.

AIDS is caused by an infection with the human immunodeficiency virus (HIV). HIV attacks selected cells in a person's immune system and suppresses the body's ability to resist harmful organisms. The body is then at risk for developing infections and certain types of cancers.

Following an HIV infection, a person may show no symptoms at all, or a mononucleosis-like illness may develop. The period between the initial HIV infection and the development of AIDS varies from six months to eleven years. Most people who are infected with the HIV virus will develop full-blown AIDS within seven years after infection. Once the person has AIDS, there is usually a rapid decline in health. Most people with

AIDS symptoms die within three years, but there have been a small number of exceptions to this.

To make the distinction between HIV and AIDS, doctors use a battery of medical tests including a laboratory test that measures the presence of certain kinds of cells.

ADVANTAGES AND DISADVANTAGES OF ANIMAL-ASSISTED THERAPY IN AN AIDS SETTING

As a person who volunteers with your pet in an AIDS setting, you can be assured that your work is very much appreciated. Unfortunately, there is still quite a social stigma associated with AIDS, and patients have very often been rejected by many people. The affection and caring that you and your animal can provide will go a long way toward helping someone have some enjoyable times.

The disadvantage of working in AIDS settings is that there is a significant amount of concern about further compromising the immune systems of patients. You will need to complete the facility's infection control training, and you might have to follow rigorous infection control procedures. This is for your own safety. Animals who visit AIDS programs may be required to undergo special, additional grooming and health checks before each visit. AIDS is an infectious disease and there are some risks associated in working in such a setting. Volunteers can minimize those risks by explicitly following infection control procedures that are outlined by each facility.

An AIDS-Related Group for Animal-Loving Volunteers

There are several groups in which volunteers can get involved to help AIDS patients and their pets. POWARS (Pet Owners With AIDS/ARC Resource Service, Inc.) is a non-profit organization of volunteers who provide pet food, supplies, veterinary care and other daily services to keep people with AIDS together with their pets. For years the program has functioned on only volunteer labor, but, in 1995, POWARS received a $25,000 grant from the New York Community Trust. The grant will enable the group to move into commercial office space and hire a part-time administrator. POWARS produces a newsletter and volunteers can get involved in helping AIDS patients care for and keep their own animals. Some POWARS volunteers provide temporary foster homes for the pets of patients who are hospitalized and unable to make other boarding arrangements. POWARS can be contacted at P.O. Box 1116, Madison Square Station, New York, NY 10159.

SAMPLE ACTIVITIES IN AIDS AND HOSPICE SETTINGS

AIDS and hospice settings will be different for you as a volunteer. In these settings, unlike others, the primary purpose of your visit will not be to teach new skills or to reduce inappropriate behavior. The primary purpose of your visits in AIDS and hospice settings will be for you and your animal to provide companionship and support. In addition, you and your animal will provide a welcome diversion to problems.

In AIDS and hospice settings, you can use your animal to:
• Provide stimulation, conversation (tell about the breed)
• Provide companionship (animal can snuggle in a bed)
• Provide sensory gratification through touch (something patients may not have access to)
• Provide comfort to caretaker or family members (the emphasis is on the patient in these settings, and caretakers and family often get overlooked)
• Be an entertaining diversion from problems (patient can learn to teach tricks)
• Distract patient from pain

If the patients have animals of their own, you may want to volunteer without yours. You can help by:
• Walking a dog
• Feeding animals
• Cleaning cages, yards
• Taking animals to the vet
• Purchasing pet food
• Grooming animals

- Assisting in finding a future placement for the animal
- Teaching the animal functional behaviors or tricks while the patient watches
- Reading an animal story
- Watching an animal video
- Setting up a birdbath and birdfeeder near the patient's window
- Planting some plants to attract butterflies (there are books on butterfly gardening)

CASE STUDY: AN AIDS PATIENT AND HIS DOG

Dan was a thirty-four-year-old special education teacher. He was bright, hard working, had tons of friends and the students and teachers at his school worshipped the ground he walked on. One evening just before Christmas, he went to run an errand. As he drove through an intersection, another driver ran a light and broadsided his car. His face was badly cut, he almost lost one eye from shards of glass that hit him in the collision and one leg had multiple fractures.

For years Dan had known that he was HIV positive. Secondary to infections and problems resulting from the car accident, Dan soon had the symptoms of AIDS. He went home to his apartment and his mother came from another state to care for him. Dan felt unable to tell his family about the AIDS. He was leading them to believe that all of his problems were a result of the car accident. As if physical pain and numerous health problems weren't enough, Dan was suffering from emotional pain.

There was one thing in Dan's life that did make him happy. He had a Miniature Dachshund named Sassy. Dan would hold Sassy when his leg caused him physical pain and he'd drift off to sleep. He would cry about having AIDS and what he knew would happen in the future. As he cried, Sassy would come to comfort him. Unaware that some dog trainers recommend this activity for people who are confined to their homes, Dan started teaching Sassy tricks. He was thrilled when he showed me she could sit up and beg.

Toward the end of his life, Dan had bills and debts owed to many, many people. Despite plenty of counseling about how "the truth can set you free," he still refused to tell his family he had AIDS.

With all of his other problems, one of the things Dan worried about the most was Sassy's future. Finally, a fellow teacher and friend who knew about the AIDS approached Dan and said she loved Sassy and would like to have her if anything happened to him. Resolving Sassy's future was a breakthrough for Dan. He realized after he had negotiated the specifics related to Sassy's future home that he could still be effective. He began to clean up the other details in his life. He told his mother and his brothers that he had AIDS. The family was loving and supportive and they cared for Dan at home until his death.

Months after Dan died, I received a letter from his mother. She enclosed a picture of a very life-like, full-size sculpture of a minia-ture black and tan Dachshund. "I thought you'd like to see the sculpture I bought," she wrote. "I have it near my fireplace. It looks just like Sassy. I like having it because when times were the bleakest for Dan, she could still make him smile. He loved teach-ing her those tricks and he seemed to rest better when Sassy was with him. Now I rest better when I think about what she did for him."

CASE STUDY: DYING WITH DIGNITY

About two years before he died, my dad had been diagnosed with a brain tumor. He had a meningioma, a slow-growing tumor that was non-malignant. He'd had one major brain surgery to remove most of the tumor and, following the surgery, it took him months to regain the ability to walk or talk. In the fall of 1994, he started falling. By Christmas, he was in a wheelchair and had problems using one arm. After seeing several doctors to get opinions, one gave us great hope. He felt that the loss of functioning was not due to the tumor, but due to pressure on the brain from fluid build-up. A simple forty-minute operation in which a shunt was installed would fix everything. I knew about shunts from my work with developmentally delayed children. The doctor was right; these days, installing a shunt was a simple procedure.

My dad came out of the forty-minute shunt operation seven hours later, paralyzed from the neck down. His face was swollen to twice its normal size, and within three days, he'd developed a severe case of pneumonia. He wasn't going to live.

The realization that I was going to lose my father was incredibly painful. It was made much more painful by the fact that he was in a hospital where many of the staff had written him off. He was being treated like a non-person. Staff would come into the room and talk about him in his presence. They would avoid eye contact with him and ask family members what he'd like to eat or how he was feeling. More than once, my response was, "He can talk, you need to ask *him*."

Of a team of four doctors, three weren't saying much and one was advocating another surgery. One doctor said we should have a family meeting with the doctors to decide my dad's fate. "Sorry," I said. "That's inappropriate. There is nothing wrong with his mind, so the choice will be his." When I asked him about his choice, my father began to sob. "Please don't make me have another surgery," he said. "It's my time to die, I want no more pain." I told him the choice was his and we would take him home for hospice care.

I explained that the care provided in a hospital or nursing home would be more intense and that hospice only came a few hours a day to support the family. He said that would be fine, he just wanted to go home. If his days were numbered, he wanted to look out the window and watch "his" birds at the birdfeeders and see the squirrels.

My dad died on April 22, 1995, at home. When it was clear he was going to die, what he wanted was to spend his last few days watching animals and nature. Some days, he could hardly breathe. But he managed to laugh at the squirrels who came to steal the food from the birdfeeders. "There's Charlie," he'd say, seeing a squirrel and smiling. For the longest time, I thought there was only one squirrel named Charlie. Then I realized there were a lot of squirrels, and he called them all Charlie. In his last days, they all made him happy.

A PARTING THOUGHT ABOUT THESE SETTINGS

If you choose to volunteer with your pet in an AIDS or hospice program, you can affect the lives of people who are in need of companionship and comfort. As a volunteer in one of these settings, you will gain much from the experience, too. People who are dying can help us become better people. They remind us that when it's time to say good-bye, what really matters are those we love and for whom we care most.

CHAPTER 13

Prisons and Detention Centers

Until the eighteenth century, prisons were places convicts were sent to receive various forms of corporal punishment or to be executed. Retribution was the primary purpose of early prison programs and the treatment of prisoners was harsh.

During the Enlightenment period in the eighteenth century, the blatant, inhumane treatment in prisons and programs for "incorrigible children" was questioned. As a result of this shift in thinking, some facilities began to teach vocational skills to prisoners and delinquents. The concept of "rehabilitation" in prisons and detention programs caught on, and eventually animal-assisted therapy was introduced within prison populations.

Perhaps the most famous recipient of animal-assisted therapy in a prison setting was the Birdman of Alcatraz. I thought the story was fictionalized until I visited Alcatraz. Today, Alcatraz stands empty and silent except for the sounds of the tourist footsteps that go through the buildings. The cell of Richard Stroud, the Birdman, is there. Before he came to Alcatraz (where he never had birds), Stroud was at Leavenworth Prison. It was there that he found some acceptance and a way in which he could be productive by studying birds in his cell and writing about bird diseases. Stroud's case shows that no matter what a person's history might be, animals can provide the will to keep on living and the desire to engage in worthwhile activity.

A MODEL PROGRAM IN A MEN'S PRISON

In 1975, David Lee, a psychiatric social worker, started this country's first organized animal-assisted therapy program at the Oakwood Forensic Center in Lima, Ohio. At the time, the Oakwood program served over 300 convicted psychopaths. Lee introduced a variety of animals to one ward in order to address problems such as depression, loneliness, boredom and low self-esteem. The animals used included rabbits, fish, gerbils, birds, deer and guinea pigs. Lee's program was a state-of-the-art animal-assisted therapy prison program.

In 1981, Lee conducted research on the program in order to validate the effects with more than stories and anecdotal reports. The results were astounding. Inmates (who were considered psychiatric patients) who had pets needed half as much medication for behavior control and there were dramatic decreases in documented aggressions toward other people.

The Oakwood program allowed prisoners to have animals to care for. Prisoners learned responsibility and were treated as though they were trusted. Animals provided a common ground on which staff and prisoners could communicate and have positive interactions. It is important to note that this program was sophisticated and well planned. A systematic behavior plan was in place that involved graduating levels of responsibility. Prisoners were given animals to care for in their cells (unsupervised) only after they had shown that they could care for one of the animals in the public courtyard in the presence of staff.

A MODEL PROGRAM IN A WOMEN'S PRISON

As David Lee was beginning to document the results of the Oakwood animal-assisted therapy program for men who were criminally insane, a pioneering program involving animals in women's

Women inmates in this program at the Purdy Treatment Center train dogs that are then adopted by the general public.
Courtesy of Delta Society

prisons was getting off the ground. Kathy Quinn (who later became Sister Pauline) was a bright, energetic person who had a love of dogs and dog training. Quinn had been in fourteen institutions herself when she had the idea of allowing inmates to train dogs to provide them with some employable skills. Quinn approached Linda Hines and Leo Bustad at Washington State University's People-Pet-Partnership program, and, with their help and guidance, a dog training program was implemented at Purdy Treatment Center for Women in 1982.

The Purdy Treatment Center, in Gig Harbor, Washington, is a maximum security women's prison. In the Purdy dog training program, inmates registered for eleven-week classes through the local community college. They learned to train and groom dogs and, at some times in the program, ran a boarding service for community dogs. The animals the inmates trained were selected from the Tacoma-Pierce County Humane Society. With training, dogs that may not have been adopted before quickly found new homes and loving owners.

When I visited Purdy, the dogs all had excellent manners and would have made wonderful pets. Some of the inmates had developed more advanced training skills and were involved in training dogs that were later placed as therapy or service animals. One inmate, Sue Miller, was involved in providing basic training to the first known dog who had the natural ability to detect seizures for the owner before they happened. Miller (who writes and conducts public interviews using her name) has been quoted as saying her dog training is one way she can make "one small contribution to society."

OTHER PRISON PROGRAMS

After the Oakwood and Purdy programs showed such amazing results, other prison programs were started. Earl Strimple, a Washington, D.C.–based veterinarian, started the People-Animals-Love (PAL) program in 1982 at a branch of a District of Columbia correctional facility located in Virginia. As a part of the PAL program, a vocational course in animal health technology was offered to inmates.

Several programs use horses in animal-assisted therapy. The New York State Department of Corrections worked with the Thoroughbred Retirement Foundation, Inc., to provide training for inmates in equine husbandry.

In Canon City, Colorado, the Colorado Wild Horse Inmate program started in 1985. The Colorado Department of Corrections teamed up with the Bureau of Land Management on a creative project involving wild horses. When Colorado had over 40,000 wild horses on the ranges that needed rescue, it was decided that inmates could train the horses so they were adoptable by the general public.

Animal-assisted therapy has been used in prisons in several states including Colorado, New Mexico, Hawaii, California, Washington, Ohio, South Carolina, Texas, Michigan, New York and Oklahoma. Prison-based animal-assisted therapy programs have also been developed and well-documented in Australia, England and Scotland.

Inmates in some prisons, like this one at the Colorado Department of Corrections facility in Canon City, train horses for adoption.
Courtesy of Delta Society

ANIMAL-ASSISTED THERAPY IN DETENTION CENTERS

Animal-assisted therapy has also been used in correctional facilities for offenders who arc minors. Some of the emotionally disturbed teenagers at the Green Chimneys program in Brewster, New York (discussed in Chapter 6), have entered the program because they've had problems in other settings following rules. The animals at Green Chimneys are used to teach responsibility and other work-related behaviors, such as showing up on time and using appropriate social skills.

Project POOCH (Positive Opportunities-Obvious Change With Hounds) is a program for male juvenile offenders living in an Oregon corrections facility. The juveniles learn to care for dogs that are provided by the local humane society. Volunteer dog trainers provide instruction in obedience training and careers working with dogs (like grooming or veterinary technician work). When the dogs are trained, they arc adopted by families in the community who meet the humane society guidelines.

SKILLS THAT CAN BE TAUGHT IN PRISONS AND DETENTION CENTERS

Usually, the goals for animal-assisted therapy in prison and detention programs are listed in very general terms such as increasing trust, improving self-esteem, providing the inmate with unconditional love and affection and providing a diversion from an otherwise boring existence in a tightly controlled environment. These goals are good, but they are not measurable. How do we know if self-esteem has improved? Is the person more trusting or not? Some specific objectives can be developed for goals such as these for animal-assisted therapy programs in prisons and detention centers. These could include:

Behavioral
- Decreasing the number of suicide threats (per month, week, etc.)
- Decreasing the number of runaway attempts (per month, week, etc.)
- Decreasing the number of times prisoner left an activity without permission (AWOL)
- Decreasing the incidents of verbal aggression
- Decreasing the incidents of physical aggression
- Decreasing the violations of specific rules (like no swearing)
- Decreasing the incidents of stealing from others
- Increasing positive verbal interactions with others
- Increasing incidents of prosocial behaviors, such as sharing

Unstructured (leisure) time
- Increasing the amount of time on a task in a selected leisure activity
- Playing with or walking the animal
- Making the choice to participate in a leisure-time activity

Vocational
- Showing up at appointed time for animal care
- Feeding and watering animals

- Cleaning pens and enclosures
- Grooming and brushing animals
- Advanced grooming (use clippers, etc.)
- Trimming nails
- Assisting vet
- Performing vet tech skills that have been taught
- Training dogs
- Training horses
- Exercising animals
- Learning knowledge related to animal care (dog breeds, etc.)

Communication/social
- Inmate writing to new owner of dog he or she has trained (with permission)
- Telling another person about the animal being cared for
- Teaching another person to care for the animal
- Writing or dictating information about the animal
- Interacting with staff about the animal; asking for help or information; reporting status of animal

VOLUNTEERING IN A PRISON OR DETENTION CENTER

So, this is the setting for you. You want to volunteer in a prison or detention center. Because of security and liability, there are not many programs that will allow volunteers to visit on a regular basis with their own pets.

There are some programs that will allow volunteers with pets. These are usually not maximum security facilities. If you take your own pet to a prison or detention center, make sure you are given adequate staff support to maintain safety for yourself and your animal at all times.

One of my colleagues took her dogs to a local residential program for delinquent boys. After several visits, the evening shift staff began to see her arrival as an opportunity for them to take a break. She was left alone with several dogs and several teenagers;

visits soon deteriorated. The boys started fighting and arguing over whose dog was best and who would get to use which leash. This was a program where the clients were on very intense behavior management programs. They earned points all through the day and had points taken away for misbehavior. In the absence of the facility staff, the boys took a holiday from behavioral programming. This situation should not have happened. It was both unsafe and poor treatment of a volunteer. Ideally, facility staff would have incorporated the volunteer and her dogs into the therapeutic program. An opportunity for the boys to engage in some positive behaviors was missed.

If you choose to volunteer at a prison or detention program that will not permit you to bring your pet, you can get involved in teaching inmates to train dogs, care for animals or learn vocational skills related to animal care.

People in prisons and detention centers experience loneliness and boredom. They no longer have any of their own possessions, and they often begin to feel personally inadequate. Animal-assisted therapy has been documented to be effective in prison and detention settings. If you choose one of these settings for volunteering with your pet, you can get involved in teaching important life lessons about caring for other living things.

CHAPTER 14

Miscellaneous Settings

Animals are being used in therapeutic settings everywhere. In addition to volunteering with your animal in traditional placements such as schools and nursing homes, there are some other settings you can visit.

Animal-assisted therapy is used in rehabilitation hospitals; shelters for abused children, battered women and homeless people; foster-care settings; settings for well elders; private homes and courtrooms.

REHABILITATION HOSPITALS

Rehabilitation hospitals serve clients who are in need of rehabilitative services that may include physical therapy, occupational therapy, speech therapy or cognitive therapy. Clients in rehabilitation hospitals may have had head injuries, spinal cord injuries or other injuries or illnesses resulting in a need for therapy.

Clients with head injuries might work on improving motor control (learning to walk after a motorcycle accident, for example), sensory functioning (like learning to deal with decreased sensation) or memory.

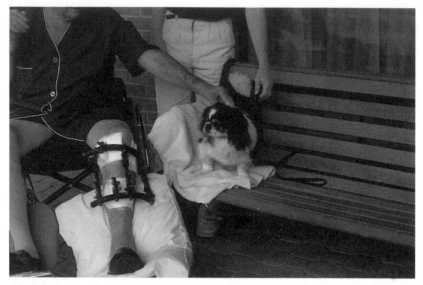

Therapy animals in rehabilitation hospitals must behave appropriately around unusual equipment.
Courtesy of Cynda Crawford, PhD, DVM, and Patty

Clients who have had spinal cord injuries work on improving motor control, sensory problems and interpersonal skills in rehabilitation hospitals.

In rehabilitation hospitals, there is often a great deal of healthcare and therapy equipment. Therapy animals in rehabilitation hospitals need to behave appropriately in the presence of unusual equipment.

THERAPY ANIMALS IN SHELTERS

In shelter programs for children or adults who have been abused, animals give unconditional love and support. In Ft. Collins, Colorado, veterinary students in Colorado State University's SHARE program (Students for Human-Animal Relationship Education) took homeless animals from the local animal shelter to visit mothers and children at a shelter. The goal of the program was to take the children's minds off their own problems and to provide the mothers and children with a positive activity they could share.

Therapists who have worked with children who are abused know that there is very often a cycle to domestic violence. Fathers beat mothers, mothers beat children and children take it all out on smaller siblings and family pets. In Macon, Georgia, at the B. Sanders Walker Center, children entering the home for battered women were given access to animals. According to program director O'Teria Mathews, after children took care of small animals such as rabbits and had the opportunity to ride horses and a llama in the petting zoo, they were less likely to hit their mothers.

FOSTER CARE

Therapy animals can be used in foster-care settings with children. Children are placed in foster care for several reasons. Some are awaiting adoption by a family. Others are receiving protective foster services because their home situation was determined to be unfit or unsafe by the courts. A third type of foster placement is a semi-permanent placement, where foster parents keep the child for a long period of time, but the adoption process is not underway. Many children in foster placement are unsettled. They are aware that there might be a major transition in their lives in the future. Volunteers with animals can provide some fun activities for the child. Very often, children in foster care will talk about their problems in the presence of animals.

SETTINGS FOR WELL ELDERS: COMMUNITY PROGRAMS AND PRIVATE HOMES

Well elders are senior citizens who may or may not receive some special services. They might continue to live in their own homes and receive a minimum of support from community programs, or they might live in a retirement community. Many older people would love to have access to an animal. They are afraid to get another pet for fear of outliving the pet. If you and your pet decide you don't want to visit a traditional therapy setting, you might want to consider working with well elders. How do you find people who would like to be visited?

In most communities, there are Area Agencies on Aging or other similar programs. Area Agencies on Aging are generally supportive of animal-assisted therapy and are involved in providing community-based services to older people. You might be able to create a role for yourself within a community-based program such as an Area Agency on Aging.

If you decide you would like to volunteer without your animal, you could help well elders with their own pets. Many older people have problems getting an animal to the veterinarian or getting to the grocery store for food. You can find out how you and your pet could help well elders by contacting an aging agency in your community. If you have a retirement community in your area, you could contact the activity director and ask if volunteers are needed. Be specific and make it clear that you would like to volunteer in a role that involved animals. Sometimes, community therapists will be aware of an older person who lives at home who could benefit from a volunteer helper. The volunteer might help by walking the person's dog, caring for the cat or cleaning the bird cage. If you get into an arrangement involving going to a private home, make sure you are covered in terms of liability insurance and documentation with an official agency.

COURTROOMS

A recent use of animal-assisted therapy has been in courtroom settings where children might be afraid to testify. Children are taught to talk to or in the presence of an animal, and when they go into court, that animal is present to provide support and stimulus control.

CASE STUDY: A DOG HELPS TREAT ELECTIVE MUTISM

There are so many contributions that you and your pet can make in animal-assisted therapy settings. The following case study describes the use of a therapy dog to treat elective mutism. Elective mutism—when a person can talk but chooses not to—is a problem that should be treated by a trained, qualified professional. It would never be appropriate for a volunteer to attempt to address a problem of this nature independently. Volunteers who happened to be trained, qualified professionals in behavior analysis, psychology or counseling could use some of the procedures described below.

Some volunteers might like to work on clinical problems, but they are not trained therapists. In these cases, volunteers can get to know a therapist and volunteer their animal-assisted therapy services. I worked with the client who is described below using my own Utility-level-trained Border Collie. Most therapists would not have access to such a dog, and if they chose to implement a similar treatment, the help of a volunteer with a trained dog would be critical.

Jason was four years old when he was referred for services. He was diagnosed as electively mute. He would speak to himself when he thought no one was listening, such as when he sat in the corner away from his family members.

On my first visit, I conducted a reinforcer assessment with Jason, which means I simply tried to find out if there was anything he liked. I tried to get him interested in toys, a music box and juice, but there was no response. When I offered Jason a cookie, he looked down and avoided eye contact.

I decided that Jason had made up his mind he had nothing to say to people, and, after several sessions, I decided to assess his reaction to a therapy dog. Jason seemed interested in my Border Collie, Laddie, but he didn't talk. At one point in a therapy session with the dog, we took a break and went outside. I decided to take advantage of the fact that young children like their possessions. I threw Jason's shoe across the yard. I told Laddie to fetch it and before he could return with the shoe, he was given a signal to turn and sit. We had Jason's attention. Quietly, I said, "Jason, he's a dog. He doesn't know what to do. If you want your shoe, tell him to come." I looked away. There were several long seconds of silence and then I heard a little voice whisper, "Come." It was Jason's first functional use of language in a long time. I signaled Laddie to come and sit in front of Jason. "Jason," I said, "He's a dog. He doesn't know what to do. If you want your shoe, say 'Give shoe.'"

"Give shoe," was his response, and we were on our way to building language. Eventually, I had Jason tell me what he wanted

Here a therapy dog works with a child who is electively mute. In the first photo, after the dog gets the child's shoe, he must say "Come." In the next, to retrieve the shoe from the dog, the child must say "Give shoe."

the dog to do (like "Find ball"). Then, Jason's sister was added to the sessions. Eight months later, individual sessions with Jason were discontinued because he was talking and doing well enough to enter a preschool program.

CASE STUDY: ASSISTING A CHILD IN FOSTER CARE

Aaron was a five-year-old child who had been placed in foster care by a protective services agency. His mother and father had long histories of alcohol and substance abuse and it was decided that the home setting was not appropriate for a young child. Aaron had curly dark hair and bronze-colored skin; he was a beautiful child. A worker at the foster home called and asked me to visit with one of my dogs.

Aaron was depressed and he was not talking to his counselor about his troubles. I took my Welsh Springer Spaniel, Sarge, on the visit. He is a reserved dog and is comfortable working with reserved people in therapy settings. Aaron and Sarge were buddies almost instantly. We all sat on the ground and Aaron began to gently pet Sarge. Sarge rolled over and offered his tummy for petting. "So how are you doing?" I asked. "Fine," was Aaron's response. "How's school?" I said. "Fine," was Aaron's response. I didn't push him to talk. We all sat for a long time saying nothing. Finally, Aaron said, "This is a beautiful dog. Where did you get him?" I explained the early childhood version of responsible breeding and how I contacted a woman who knew so much about these dogs and I waited almost a whole year for a puppy. "There's another place to get a dog," Aaron said. He then told me about the animal shelter. He saw it when his family took the pets to the shelter a few days before dropping Aaron off to be placed in foster care. The similarity of Aaron and the family pets was too close. I blinked back tears and forced myself to keep my emotions under control.

At the age of five, Aaron had seen a lot and was wise for his years. He, too, had some level of understanding of a culture where children and animals are expendable. "The animal shelter is a nice place," he continued. "They feed the animals and they give them water, and they stay inside. But it is really sad because nobody wants the animals at the shelter and they don't have a family to love them." It was quite clear that Aaron was talking about himself. He was in a foster placement where he was given a bedroom and good food. What he wanted was a family. Aaron was not ready to talk to a counselor who was asking direct, difficult questions. When he talked about the therapy dog and dogs he knew about in the world, he could make his own feelings easily understood.

CASE STUDY: A THERAPY DOG FOR A WELL ELDER

Sam was a well elder who was on his way to becoming a not-so-well elder when he was referred for services. Sam was seventy-five years old. His wife had died, his adult children had moved away and the grandchildren were too busy to contact Sam. Sam was clinically depressed. He had become withdrawn and stayed in his house with the curtains closed most of the time. There was not much to do in the house except watch television and eat. Sam developed a weight problem that was accompanied by high blood pressure. His doctors were considering putting him on medications for blood pressure and depression, but decided to try behavioral therapy first.

The first thing that was done was to conduct a reinforcer assessment. With someone like Sam, it was possible to be very direct. "Look," I said, "Your family is worried sick about you. Is there anything you would like to do or in which you could get involved?" Sam let me know in a hurry he wanted no part of the outside world. Weeks later, when he was talking about his fondness for animals, I said, "Well, if you don't want to go out, we could get some things for you to do here. Would you ever consider owning another animal?" He thought about it and then he told me he wanted a dog. I was ecstatic. "Wow—this is great, I could help you find a nice small dog." Sam quickly reminded me that I'd forgotten all about choice. "Nope, no small dogs for me," he said. "I want a Doberman." Sam had been a Doberman Pinscher man all his life. He knew what was involved in caring for a larger dog and he was ready to give it a try.

We found a Doberman Pinscher and a volunteer who was willing to provide basic canine good citizen training. Within weeks, Sam had Brutus. It was Brutus who was responsible for Sam's therapy. When Brutus arrived, the curtains were opened again. Brutus liked walks, so Sam took him all through the neighborhood twice a day. Sam started talking to his neighbors again because Brutus gave him something to talk about. Brutus was well-trained but assertive enough regarding his walks that Sam lost weight. His blood pressure was down within three months and no medications were needed. Sam was a well elder living in his home in the community. Depression is common among older people living alone. Brutus provided the companionship that Sam needed to feel that he had a purpose and someone to share things with. "He's well trained," he told me. "I can take him anywhere. I know that he needs me, and I know I need him."

Volunteers who are interested in well elders could help clients like Sam by providing support services to the person and their pet. Volunteers can help with training, walking or bathing pets. In cases where the person is not quite ready to take on the responsibility of pet ownership, volunteers can visit with their own animals at regularly scheduled times.

CHAPTER 15

Non-Therapeutic Settings

The primary focus of this book has been to present opportunities for volunteering with pets in therapy settings. In addition to therapy environments, there are other settings where volunteers and their pets can make a contribution.

HUMANE EDUCATION

Common goals of humane-education programs are to teach kindness toward animals, responsible pet ownership, concepts pertaining to animal shelters and animal control and basic pet care. Humane-education programs are most often offered by animal shelters, animal-welfare organizations and animal-control agencies. Many of these agencies have limited resources, but a few are fortunate enough to have all of the funding and resources needed for a comprehensive humane-education program.

PRE-KINDERGARTEN AND ELEMENTARY CURRICULA

As a volunteer, you and your pet can help in your community's humane-education efforts. Some volunteers work with shelters or humane societies to make presentations to local schools and community groups. Children of all ages can benefit from lessons that relate to animals. In pre-kindergarten programs, a volunteer with a guinea pig can teach children very basic concepts such as animal identification. "What is this? That's right. It's a guinea pig." Pre-kindergarten and kindergarten children can learn about basic animal care and that animals have many of the same needs as we do.

Children as young as kindergarten age can begin learning concepts related to responsible pet ownership. As a volunteer, if you visit a classroom with your own pet, you'll be able to describe the things you do to keep your pet safe and healthy. Even if you do not have experience teaching children, you'll be amazed at how quickly children will guide you into talking about critical issues in the animal world. A child's comment, "I'd like to have a monkey," can lead to a stimulating and informative discussion about whether or not wild animals really make good pets.

Concepts that relate to pet overpopulation and animal welfare can be introduced to third and fourth graders, and fifth and sixth graders can understand and participate in discussions about animal welfare.

Students in high school and adults are not too old for humane-education programs. In high school, humane education ties in well with civics class and the concept of social responsibility. High school students are one step away from entering the world as adults who live on their own and can choose to own animals.

Whatever the age of the audience, if you have a pet that you can take with you on a visit, topics can relate to your pet. "This is my dog. I'd like to show you some things he can do," could be the introduction on the importance of teaching dogs basic good manners.

Teachers report they don't do more humane education in the schools because the materials are not readily available. If you work with a local group such as an animal-control agency, you might be able to borrow materials. Other excellent sources of materials for humane-education programs are below.

SOURCES FOR HUMANE-EDUCATION MATERIALS

1. **American Humane Association** (AHA), 9725 East Hampden Ave., Denver, CO 80231. The AHA has a complete catalog and extensive materials on topics such as different species of animals, pet overpopulation, how to avoid dog bites and caring for pets in classrooms.
2. **American Kennel Club,** 51 Madison Ave., New York, NY 10010. The American Kennel Club (AKC) has many pamphlets on care, selection, training and breeding of dogs. The AKC has an education department that can assist you in obtaining materials including information on the Canine Good Citizen program and the *Taking Care of Corey* children's program about dogs and responsibility.
3. **ASPCA Education Department,** 441 East 92nd St., New York, NY 10128. The ASPCA has training materials for a variety of humane-education topics.
4. **Humane Society of the United States** (HSUS), 2100 L St. NW, Washington, DC 20037. The Humane Society also has an extensive catalog including written and audio-visual materials.

DEMONSTRATIONS AT SCHOOLS AND COMMUNITY EVENTS

If you would like to go to schools or community groups with your pet but prefer to do something other than humane education, you can give demonstrations with your pet. Dogs can perform obedience routines and tricks. Cats and other small animals can be used to teach people about a particular species, breed or type of animal.

Volunteers can choose to work with their pets on special community projects such as establishing Responsible Pet Ownership Neighborhoods. These types of neighborhoods have been started in several states. Volunteers work with established neighborhood

Volunteers can work on special projects such as Responsible Pet Ownership Neighborhoods. Here, Sgt. Duane Pickel poses with Champion Tailgate's George von Pickel, UD (Utility Dog).

associations to provide training to residents on responsible pet ownership. Neighborhood residents are trained at meetings where volunteers with pets can come and talk about specific topics.

SHARING YOUR PET WITH OTHER ANIMALS

If your pet is good around other animals, you may wish to get involved in training or raising another animal. Some service dog organizations need puppy raisers and volunteers who can provide a future service dog with an early education.

Rescue league animals will often go to a home with other pets. You and your pet can get involved in rehabilitating a rescue animal. Rescued track Greyhounds make wonderful pets, but they need to learn to live with cats and small animals. Many sporting dogs and guard breeds will be adopted only if they can get along with another family pet. Working with animals who are in need of homes is one more way that you and your pet can volunteer. If you are interested in working with a rescue league animal, the American Kennel Club, at 51 Madison Ave., New York, NY 10010, can provide you with a list of breed rescue organizations.

VOLUNTEERING WITHOUT YOUR PET

There might be a time when you want to volunteer in a setting with animals without your pet. You may want to begin volunteering on your own if your pet does not pass the necessary screening. It is never appropriate to continue using an animal for therapy work who is not enjoying the work. At the first signs of ongoing burnout or aging problems, your pet should be retired.

When you retire your therapy animal, there are other activities that you can do with your pet to have fun and quality time together. You can continue to volunteer in a number of settings with animals.

You can always continue your animal-assisted therapy visits without your pet. You may also begin visiting with another volunteer and offer to help record client progress, plan activities, evaluate animals or train new volunteers.

If you need a change of pace, many communities have zoos, aquariums and museums with extensive programs for volunteers.

NATIONAL VOLUNTEER WORK AT ANIMAL PROGRAMS

There are some exciting opportunities nationally if you are willing to travel to do some short-term volunteer work. Wolf Park, in Battleground, Indiana, needs volunteers who are willing to devote a few weeks as "puppy mothers" (or fathers.) Volunteers stay at Wolf Park and sign up for round-the-clock shifts bottle-feeding baby wolves.

At Dolphins Plus in Key Largo, Florida, volunteers can work with dolphins in a program designed to rehabilitate physically challenged children. Dolphins Plus provides animal-assisted therapy in the true sense of the term. Goals and objectives are written for each child. Two main treatment areas for the children are physical strength and stamina as well as self-confidence. Dolphins Plus can be contacted at: Dolphins Plus, P.O. Box 2728, Key Largo, FL 33037.

Helping Others Learn About Animal-Assisted Therapy

There are many opportunities for volunteers who want to help others learn about animal-assisted therapy. Local 4-H groups often welcome volunteers to work with children on projects. Children can be taught about animal-assisted therapy through classes that prepare them and their pets for work in a therapy setting. Several 4-H groups work on Canine Good Citizen training.

Boy Scout and Girl Scout troops are often in need of volunteers. Scouts can earn merit badges for community service and animal care. Advanced scouting awards such as the Eagle Scout Award require that the scout complete a fairly large-scale community project. You could volunteer to serve as the "major advisor" to a scout who organized some therapy dog demonstrations or a Canine Good Citizen Test at a community event.

You can choose to volunteer with or without an animal. You can choose to volunteer in a therapy setting or in a community setting. Whatever direction you decide to take, with proper training, preparation and commitment on the part of you and your pet, your opportunities for success and making a difference in the lives of others are endless.

PART IV
Off on Your Own

CHAPTER 16

Putting a Program Together

If you choose to simply visit a facility with your pet, you will be involved in animal-assisted activities. You and your animal might give demonstrations or you might simply talk to clients during your visits.

Animal-assisted activities are basic "meet and greet" activities that occur when volunteers and their pets visit clients. Generally, no treatment goals for clients have been identified in these visits. By contrast, in animal-assisted therapy, volunteers and their pets work on goals that have been determined by facility professionals. There is a written record of client progress, and professional staff (such as physical therapists) maintain a working relationship with the volunteer as the program proceeds.

Rather than always doing animal-assisted activities, you might want to get involved in animal-assisted therapy, where there are goals and objectives for clients and progress is measured. If you choose to participate in animal-assisted therapy, the work should always be done under the direction of a facility professional!

If you have no background as a therapist or human services professional and you want to try animal-assisted therapy, begin gradually. Start with one or two clients and involve all of the others in animal-assisted activities until you have developed some skills. Remember that you should be working closely with a facility staff person or trained professional. A plan for getting started in animal-assisted therapy follows.

PLANNING AN ANIMAL-ASSISTED THERAPY PROGRAM FOR AN INDIVIDUAL CLIENT

1. Get facility approval and identify a professional who will work with you.

The first step is officially to enlist the support of the facility and a professional who will work with you. You can go to the facility contact person and explain that you would like to get involved in helping some clients reach some treatment objectives. Ask if there is a professional who would be willing to work with you.

Suggested professionals might be an occupational therapist, who could use your animal in working with a client to improve fine motor (hand) skills; a physical therapist, who might be willing to use you and your dog in a walking program for a client; a speech therapist, who might teach a client to say words to your parrot; or a recreational therapist, who could have clients play ball with your therapy dog.

Depending on the nature of the goal and the client's problems, the facility professional might always be present and assume a primary role in therapy sessions. In other cases, your professional contact may train you to run the program and check with you on progress periodically.

The amount of time the professional spends with you will vary. Whatever is decided, remember that, as a volunteer, you are not qualified to plan therapy programs or determine goals and objectives. For both liability and ethical reasons, you *must* work with a professional.

In some cases, professionals may not have the time to work with volunteers. If no one in the facility is willing to work with you, you have two choices. You can do animal-assisted activities or you can request a placement at a facility where therapy is a priority and the potential contribution of volunteers is recognized.

2. Conduct a reinforcer assessment.

A reinforcer is, in scientific terms, "a stimulus following a response that increases the likelihood a response will occur again." A positive reinforcer is something a person likes and will work for. Food and money are examples of positive reinforcers. A reinforcer assessment is a procedure that can be used to determine if a person likes something that is presented, such as a certain kind of music or a therapy animal.

For many individuals, finding out if they like something is a simple process. You simply ask them, "Do you like cats?" and, if the person can answer you, this will give you the information you need. When Luella said, "Get that dog out of this room!" I didn't need to fill out a reinforcer assessment to discover that she didn't like dogs.

Sometimes, you will work with clients who cannot express their feelings verbally. Such clients might include elderly people who no longer talk, children who are electively mute or individuals with profound retardation and no speech. In such cases, you can use a reinforcer assessment to determine if the person likes your animal. To conduct a reinforcer assessment, you can record the client's responses to your animal. Client behaviors such as smiling, reaching out to pet the animal, talking to the animal or attempting to get closer to the animal can indicate that the client likes the animal. If you present your animal and the client turns away, grimaces or cries, the client may not like animals. Remember that all clients have the right to make choices about spending time with pets.

3. Determine goals and objectives for the program.

You have identified a facility professional who will work with you. You feel certain that the client likes your pet. With the facility professional, the next step is to determine the goals and objectives of your animal-assisted therapy program. Remember that in most facilities, clients have treatment plans. The facility professional can talk to you about reasonable goals for a particular client based on the client's treatment plan.

REINFORCER ASSESSMENT FOR ANIMAL-ASSISTED THERAPY

Client_____

Observer_____

Date_____

	APPEARS TO LIKE ANIMAL								APPEARS TO NOT LIKE ANIMAL							SHOWS NO RESPONSE
	Looks at animal	Laughs or smiles re: animal	Reaches for animal	Increases body or facial activity	Vocalizes [happy sounds]	Verbalizes "I like the dog"	Touches/pets		Jerks away/turns face away	Cries, frowns	Grimaces	Stiffens body	Frightened vocalizing	Verbalizes "I'm afraid"		Shows no response or tolerates the animal
Animal:																
Trial 1																
Trial 2																
Trial 3																
Animal:																
Trial 1																
Trial 2																
Trial 3																
Animal:																
Trial 1																
Trial 2																
Trial 3																

Goals are more broad and general than objectives. A goal might be, "The child will learn to walk independently." Objectives are more specific and break the task into smaller components to make instruction easier. An objective would be, "The child will stand for thirty seconds while holding onto a therapy dog." To measure the progress, the length of time the child stood in each trial would be recorded.

4. Plan the therapy program.

With the help of the facility professional, after you determine goals and objectives, it is time to write the therapy program. Using the first objective, you can develop a task analysis of the behavior. A task analysis is simply a breakdown of the task into smaller parts. For the objective, "the child stands for thirty seconds while holding onto a therapy dog," the following task analysis might be used.

   a. Child stands for five seconds while holding onto a therapy dog. (We would assume the child and dog were matched for size, such as a toddler with a Golden Retriever.)
   b. Child stands for ten seconds while holding onto a therapy dog.
   c. Child stands for fifteen seconds while holding onto a therapy dog.
   d. Child stands for twenty seconds while holding onto a therapy dog.
   e. Child stands for thirty seconds while holding onto a therapy dog.

When a client performs all steps of the task analysis, it is time to start on the next objective. If the client has trouble learning a particular step of the task analysis, it is too difficult and needs to be broken into smaller steps. If the client performs all of the steps in the first session, the task analysis or the objective was too easy. You can put the steps of the task analysis on a form and record the client's progress in each session.

DATA COLLECTION

Month_____ Year 199___

TASK ANALYSIS																
1. Holds head up																
2. Looks at dog																
3. Remains upright																
4. Reaches to dog																
5. Touches dog																
initials																

CODE: A = Independent
        B = Verbal Cue
        C = Modeling
        D = Physical Assist
        E = Not Met

5. Record the client progress and continue to evaluate effectiveness.

In order to document client progress visually, you can make a graph or record the progress in case notes. In some cases, the facility professional might wish to record the client's progress in the therapy program. If the client is having problems performing a certain task, you may need to change the goal or objective. The facility professional can help you decide this.

The basic steps to planning a therapy program where results are documented were provided so that you understand the process. If the whole process looks too complex and more than you bargained for, you may wish to do animal-assisted activities. Or, you may choose to work with a professional who will do all of the program planning and will simply tell you when to bring your animal.

If you would like to get involved in a therapy program but find the procedures complex, remember that the facility professional who is your contact should have a major role in designing any therapy program in which you are involved.

ORGANIZING A LOCAL THERAPY GROUP

You started at the beginning of the book. You and your pet got certified and you joined a national organization. You chose a therapy setting and you've been visiting for several months now. All of your friends are excited about your successes and now they want to get involved. It's time to expand and build a local program. Where do you begin? If you belong to a national organization with chapters, you can form a chapter. Contact the national organization for more information on doing this. The primary benefit of having a national organization help you formally establish a local therapy group is that you will not have to re-create the wheel. The national organization can send you the forms and the paperwork models you need to get started. To form a local group, you'll need to start with a systematic plan.

PLAN FOR FORMING A LOCAL THERAPY GROUP

1. Assess your resources.

How many volunteers will you have to help you? Volunteers can be found through local dog clubs, animal clubs and similar groups.

Are the volunteers certified? If not, assist them in getting the information they need to get certified.

Decide if you should form a group, start a chapter or start a group under someone else's program, such as through your local humane society.

2. Assess the need in your community.

How many facilities are in your community?

Do you know of any that would like animal-assisted therapy services?

If you have a lot of people who want to volunteer, survey potential volunteers to find out their desired placements. If they all choose schools, there is no point in contacting every nursing home in town to ask if they want services. An exception would be if you were committed to finding a way to provide the service to facilities that were interested. Decide if you should survey facilities to find out if they want services.

3. Plan for regular contact.

Effective therapy groups have some means of regular contact with volunteers. Decide if you are going to have weekly work sessions with dogs, monthly meetings or social time for volunteers.

4. Make decisions regarding organization.

How often do you want your volunteers to make visits?
How long are the visits?
Should they visit alone or in teams?

What are the basic goals of your local program?

Do you want volunteers to keep any data or will that be determined by the facility?

Who should the volunteers contact (in the therapy group) and what is the procedure for helping a volunteer with a problem?

Does each facility have a contact person who is responsive to the program and willing to help volunteers? Who is it?

5. Paperwork details should be in order.

Is any further insurance required?

Do you have records of volunteer and animal certification?

Current rabies and other immunization records should be on file for all animals?

Has each facility signed a facility contract to ensure that both parties understand their roles and responsibilities?

Have volunteers been trained on any local laws, health codes and policies?

6. Begin assigning volunteers to facilities.

Once volunteers are placed at facilities, they should be monitored periodically by someone in the therapy program and given feedback that is positive as well as constructive! Monitoring plan: How often/by whom?

Volunteer training and in service should be provided to all volunteers in order to further advance their skills. Training can be aimed at the volunteer or the therapy animal. Training plan: Dates/topics

Do You Know What You're Getting into?

The responsibilities of organizing and managing a local therapy group are enormous if done correctly. Staff management and administrative skills are required. Most quality programs have coordinators who put in a minimum of twenty hours per week even if they are volunteering.

There is an extremely high turnover rate in animal-assisted therapy. In order to keep volunteers, contact and feedback are needed on a regular basis. Otherwise, many volunteers feel isolated and unappreciated. We would like to think that the reinforcement in animal-assisted therapy would come from seeing clients enjoy the animals, but for most volunteers that is not enough. Volunteers are special people. They will work long and hard for no money, but need assurance that their work is appreciated. Simple recognition such as the volunteer's and animal's name or story in a newsletter goes a long way.

The work you do as an individual who volunteers with a pet is very important. When you get to the point that you are involved in organizing others for animal-assisted therapy work, you are making a different kind of special contribution. You will be rewarded with knowing that you are making a lasting contribution by getting involved in the professional development of others. Indirectly, you will be helping many, many clients receive the unconditional love and affection that only an animal can provide.

CHAPTER 17

In the Not-Too-Distant Future

When Pliny the Elder described the role of dogs in ancient Rome, he said, ". . . even when they are exhausted with old age and blind and weak, men carry them in their arms sniffing at the breezes and scents and pointing their muzzles towards cover." Even centuries ago pets were important parts of our lives and those who loved animals went out of their way to include them in daily activities.

They say that the best predictor of future behavior is past behavior. If the past is any indicator, we can assume that in future times, our animals will be there with us. What does the future hold for animal-assisted therapy and our relationship with pets?

MORE THERAPY ORGANIZATIONS

The field of animal-assisted therapy is changing daily. While there used to be only one or two organizations from which to choose, the latest trend seems to be toward increasing competition. Some groups that once filled a local need are attempting to make it as national organizations. Volunteers will have to choose wisely and be well-educated about the various aspects of the field. Therapy groups will have to work harder to maintain financial stability if volunteers and members decrease due to competition.

INCREASED PROFESSIONALISM
AND HIGHER STANDARDS

In the immediate future, as the numbers of people participating in animal-assisted therapy increase rapidly, there will undoubtedly be a need for increased professionalism and higher standards.

Since I began work in this field in 1985, I've seen many poorly behaved, untrained animals involved in therapy work. I've also seen badly trained volunteers involved in therapy work. I've seen a volunteer attach her Siberian Huskies to wheelchairs to give rides to clients. Not just rides, but fast rides. When elderly people are whizzing by attached to a team of dogs that appear to have escaped from the Iditarod, you just know there's an accident waiting to happen. Sadly, in the not-too-distant future, as the participation in animal-assisted therapy increases, so will the accidents and insurance claims. When accidents and insurance claims increase, there will certainly be an increase in the number of facilities that ban volunteers with pets. The importance of maintaining high standards for professional behavior and safety cannot be over-emphasized.

INCREASED TRAINING OPPORTUNITIES

Some colleges offer course work in animal-assisted therapy, and more courses are being developed. Some states now pay for the services of animal-assisted therapists. In the not-too-distant future, as more professionals realize the therapeutic benefits of animals, we can expect to see additional opportunities for training and certification and more agencies that are willing to pay for animal-assisted therapy services.

CLIENT CHOICE

A current hot topic in nursing homes and developmental disabilities, rehabilitation and education settings is "client choice." Federal standards for facilities serving people who have developmental disabilities require that facilities demonstrate that clients are given choices regarding dietary selections, training routines and preferences for daily recreational activities. This is an age of client-empowerment. In many states, clients have the right to choose and release from service their case managers and service coordinators. They can decide which services they would like to have purchased. As this trend continues, and more clients decide that they like animals, there will be an even greater need for animal-assisted therapy services.

LEGISLATION

The laws pertaining to ways in which we can have animals and the conditions under which we can have them are changing. There are now "Canine Good Citizen neighborhoods," and several states have Canine Good Citizen legislation. Current legislation proposes to let senior citizens in federally subsidized housing have pets. Research shows that survivors of heart attacks who have pets live longer than survivors who have no pets. As more people are aware of these and related findings, people who were once restricted from animal ownership will be able to share their lives with a pet.

Population estimates suggest that a significant percentage of our population will be over the age of sixty-five by the year 2020. As more people recognize the benefits animals can have in the lives of senior citizens, pet ownership may be encouraged and there might be an increase in programs that assist older people in owning pets. The Purina Pets for People Program provides such a model; in this program, shelter animals are screened and placed with senior citizens. The program pays for the animals' veterinary care and food.

AN INCREASING REVERENCE FOR LIFE

Leo Bustad, DVM, wrote about a concept called "the reverence for life." We need to teach children in our culture how to have a reverence for life and to respect all living things. We can do that by increasing humane-education programs in our schools and communities. We can support efforts for animals such as animal shelters, humane organizations and rescue leagues.

The importance of working with children when they are young cannot be stressed enough. Numerous studies show that serial killers abused animals as children. Too often, our well-intended efforts to provide humane education to adults arrive too late.

THE NEED FOR MORE STUDIES

One criticism of the field of animal-assisted therapy by people in other professions is that it is not research-based and there are few empirical studies to support claims that animals have therapeutic benefits. As we move into the future, the numbers of data-based studies are increasing. Hopefully, it will not be long before most settings that previously resisted having animals (such as hospitals) will recognize that the benefits of having them far outweigh the risks.

In order for animal-assisted therapy to be taken seriously, the researchers have quite a job to do. In 1993, a task force of the American Psychological Association began to develop criteria for determining if particular treatment was, by research standards, effective. The term "effectiveness" in research standards means a lot more than "the clients smiled and enjoyed the dogs." The definition is very explicit and involves research concepts like statistical power and experimental design. While this may not pertain to you as a volunteer, the important thing to know is that the task force's "Criteria for Empirically Validated Treatments" can be easily applied to animal-assisted therapy. These criteria can be used to guide the researchers who work in animal-assisted therapy. The implications of all of this for volunteers is that once a treatment has been determined to be effective, the procedures can be put in place to begin paying for the delivery of the services.

THE INFORMATION SUPERHIGHWAY AND PETS

As we move into the future, more people will be using computers and modems to work at home. This will mean people will spend more time with their pets and less time around other people. Animal-assisted therapy will be a good activity for pet owners as a means of lessening their own isolation.

The computer network is already up and running. Pet forums, Canine Good Citizen discussion groups and animal-assisted therapy discussions can be found on the computer. The New York–New England Canine Good Citizen Compuserve group recently got together in Saratoga, New York, to meet each other face to face and conduct a CGC test. As more people get to know each other through computers, we'll see events similar to the one the Saratoga group planned.

Through electronic mail (e-mail), computers will make it possible for animal-assisted therapists to stay updated to issues in the field. If a volunteer is visiting a nursing home and needs advice about a client in the advanced stages of Alzheimer's, people who have done animal-assisted therapy with similar clients can provide some tips. Volunteers will suddenly have immediate access to national experts in the field. Of course, if computers are used in this context, training programs for volunteers will have to stress issues such as confidentiality and client rights.

GOING WHERE NO ANIMAL HAS GONE BEFORE

Outside of the setting of animal-assisted therapy, as we become more technologically advanced, people are finding more creative ways to spend time with their pets. One dog on television wears his very own scuba gear to go diving with his owner. Other divers have replicated the equipment and we now have a number of scuba-diving dogs. If the time comes that we spend time in submarines or in bubbles under the ocean, animal lovers who are involved in these experiments will no doubt find a way to include their pets.

We're continuing to make advances in outer space. The people who have the mental horsepower to launch a spacecraft are no different than the rest of us in that they love their pets. Deke Slayton was a member of the Mercury Seven. He was one of America's original astronauts and was involved in America's effort to reach the moon from the very beginning. Slayton would go to the desert to watch other pilots flying over Edwards Air Force Base. He would stand and gaze at the heavens and think about the stars and the planets. And as he did that, he was not alone. He chose to share those moments with his dog, Ace. In 1995, when astronaut Norm Thagard returned from the longest journey yet to outer space, he was asked what he thought about as he circled Earth. He said he thought about his family and his cats. In the more distant future, if we have stations in outer space, we'll probably have our pets there with us.

DISNEY'S ROLE IN SUPPORTING PETS

Walt Disney has always recognized the important role of pets in our lives. In 1964, Disney opened the GE Carousel of Progress at the New York World's Fair. The attraction was Disney's own idea and was billed as having given "more performances than any stage show in the history of American theater." Today, there is a Carousel of Progress in Tomorrowland at Walt Disney World. Visitors on the ride can watch an American family go through the twentieth century with a number of changes.

The first scene shows a family at the turn of the century. There were 8,000 cars in the United States then. It took seven days to get from New York to California, and two flighty brothers in North Carolina had an idea that they could make a contraption that could fly. As the scene closes, beneath the glow of kerosene and gas lights, we see the family dog.

The second scene is twenty years later. Lindbergh was getting ready to cross the Atlantic. They were building arenas called sports stadiums and the finer homes were beginning to install indoor plumbing. And under the new electric lights, we see the family dog.

The third scene tells about how the current generation of the family is involved in commuting. Still attentive throughout the discussion is the family dog.

Finally, as the family approaches the year 2000, all of their appliances and lights are operated by voice commands. Grandma and Grandson play an exciting game using headgear and handsets for Virtual Reality. And, of course, present for it all is this generation's family dog. That wonderful dog blinks, wags his tail and gives the audience a big dog smile. The lights go out as you hear the theme song, "There's a great big beautiful tomorrow, and tomorrow is just a dream away."

CONCLUSIONS

Our feelings and hearts have told us for centuries that animals can make a difference in our lives. Now, research is beginning to experimentally demonstrate that those beliefs were absolutely correct. Animals can be used to teach new skills, increase social interaction and physical activity and have a positive effect on physiological factors like blood pressure and heart rate.

This is an incredibly exciting time for the field of animal-assisted therapy. Those of us who volunteer with our pets now will someday be able to say, "Remember when some facilities wouldn't allow animals? Remember when they didn't even have standards for animal-assisted therapists? Remember when some people actually believed that animal-assisted therapy didn't work?"

If you decide to volunteer with your pet, you'll have fun with your pet, you'll help other people and your own life will be greatly enriched.

Glossary

AAA See Animal-Assisted Activities.

AAT See Animal-Assisted Therapy.

Adaptive Behaviors The ability to change your behavior to improve your chance for survival. Learning from your experience is adaptive behavior; adaptive behavior does not generally pertain to academics and things learned in a classroom.

AIDS Acquired Immunodeficiency Syndrome. A condition caused by a virus which affects a person's immune system. AIDS results in a variety of infections, some forms of cancer and the degeneration of the nervous system.

Alpha Affiliates An all volunteer, nonprofit organization that focuses on education and science involving human–animal interactions.

Alzheimer's Disease An incurable degenerative disease of the brain. Alzheimer's causes progressive dementia and the primary symptom is memory loss.

Animal-Assisted Activities (AAA) Activities done with a volunteer and animal that are "meet and greet" activities. There is not necessarily any record of client progress and volunteers often conduct activities without the direction of facility staff.

Animal-Assisted Therapy (AAT)   AAT involves an animal and volunteer working with a facility professional. There are goals and objectives for clients and written documentation of client progress. Trained professionals with credentials in their respective fields might also conduct AAT using their own animals or facility animals.

Anthrozoos   The scientific research–oriented journal of the Delta Society. The journal addresses issues pertaining to the human–animal bond.

Autism   A disability that primarily affects an individual's language and social abilities.

Bustad, Leo   President Emeritus of the Delta Society; a leader in the human–animal bond area.

Butrick, Jack and Ann   Founders of Therapy Dogs Incorporated, an animal-assisted therapy group based in Cheyenne, Wyoming.

Canine Good Citizen (CGC)   Canine Good Citizen Test or CGC Program. The CGC Program is the American Kennel Club Program that deals with responsible dog ownership and basic good manners for dogs. The CGC Test is a ten item test of basic good manners. The test is used as a screening tool for several animal-assisted therapy groups.

Cerebral Palsy   A condition in which brain damage either before or during birth causes some degree of paralysis.

Code of Ethics   Guidelines of ethical conduct for professionals, paraprofessionals or volunteers who work in a specific area.

Cognitive   Thought processes related to knowledge, perception, memory and judgment.

Daily Living   In therapy settings, daily living skills pertain to abilities needed in daily life such as housekeeping skills, cooking and taking care of one's property and pets.

Delta Society   A nonprofit organization started in 1977. Delta's focus is increasing recognition of the mutually nurturing relationship between people and animals.

Dementia   The loss of mental abilities to the extent of interfering with normal social or everyday functioning. Memory, judgment, abstract thought and overall personality are changed.

Developmental Disabilities   Disabilities which affect normal mental or physical development; developmental disabilities include mental retardation, cerebral palsy and autism.

Elective Mutism   A condition where a person has the ability to talk but does not.

Endorphins   The body's natural pain suppressors. Endorphins are peptides (compounds formed by amino acids) that are secreted in the brain. They have a pain-relieving effect like morphine. When we stroke animals, endorphins are released.

Evaluator   In animal-assisted therapy, an evaluator is a person who has been certified or approved to certify animals for therapy work.

Fine Motor   Movements involving small muscles such as finger movements.

Foster Care   Home in which children or adults are cared for by people other than their natural family. Children may stay in foster care until they are adopted. Adults may have long-term or permanent foster care placements. Animals awaiting adoption from shelters may also be placed in foster families until homes are found.

Green Chimneys   An internationally recognized animal-assisted therapy program in Brewster, New York, that was founded by Sam Ross in 1948.

Gross Motor   Movements involving the large muscles such as those of the arms and legs.

Hippotherapy   From the Greek word *eohippos,* meaning horse. Hippotherapy is therapeutic horseback riding directed by trained professionals in areas such as physical therapy or occupational therapy.

HIV Human immunodeficiency virus. The virus attacks selected cells in the immune system and suppresses the body's ability to resist harmful organisms. AIDS follows HIV.

Hospice An alternative to hospital treatment; a hospice provides a homelike facility or treatment at home and provides supportive care for people who are terminally ill.

Humane Education Education pertaining to the humane treatment of animals; many humane-education programs stress responsible pet ownership. Goals of humane-education programs include teaching kindness toward animals, responsible pet ownership, animal control and animal population issues and basic pet care.

Inclusion Pertaining to people with disabilities, inclusion means fully including people with disabilities in the same activities as people without disabilities. This applies to community activities, educational settings, public transportation, etc.

Katcher, Aaron, MD In the early 1980s Dr. Katcher, made national news with a study at the University of Pennsylvania that showed contact with an animal could lower the blood pressure of people with hypertension.

Levinson, Dr. Boris A clinical psychologist at Yeshiva University in New York City. In the 1950s Levinson made advances in AAT when he brought his dog, Jingles, to therapy sessions and got results from children who had been previously unresponsive.

Liability Insurance In animal-assisted therapy settings, insurance that protects volunteers for their actions while volunteering.

Mental Retardation The three characteristics of mental retardation are: significant subaverage general intellectual functioning, impairments in adaptive behavior and onset of the condition during the childhood years. IQ scores are below 70.

Pet-Facilitated Therapy Therapy involving the use of an animal. The term "animal-assisted therapy" began to replace pet-facilitated therapy when professionals in the field saw a need to emphasize that not simply any "pet" was suitable for therapy work. Further, in some programs, farm animals are the therapy animals and these are not "pets."

Pet Partners Program   The Delta Society program that registers human–animal teams for volunteering in therapeutic settings. The Pet Partners Program started in 1990 and is a part of the Delta Society. The Delta Society has offices in Renton, Washington, and New York City.

Pet Therapy   This term is sometimes used to refer to therapy involving the use of an animal. The preferred term is animal-assisted therapy. Professionals in the field make the case that not any "pet" is suitable for therapy work. Pet therapy was also first used in the literature to describe the work animal behaviorists do with pets who have behavior problems. Traditionally, pet therapy is behavior therapy for pets.

Phobia   An irrational, excessive or persistent fear of something or some situation. Some people have animal phobias.

POWARS   Pet Owners with AIDS/ARC Resource Service, Inc. A nonprofit organization for volunteers who provide pet food, supplies, veterinary care and other daily services to keep people with AIDS together with their pets.

PPAT   Pet Partners Aptitude Test. The screening tool for evaluating the "temperament" of potential therapy animals for the Delta Society Pet Partners Program. The test is basically a simulated therapy visit.

PPST   Pet Partners Skills Test. The screening tool for evaluating basic trained behaviors or "good manners" of potential therapy animals for the Delta Society Pet Partners Program. The test is basically a modified version of the American Kennel Club's Canine Good Citizen Test.

Rehabiliation Hospital (Rehab hospital)   Hospital for patients in need of services that may include physical therapy, occupational therapy, speech therapy or cognitive therapy. Rehab hospitals treat patients with head injuries, spinal cord injuries, etc.

Reinforcer   A stimulus following a response that increases the likelihood the response will occur again. In therapy settings, positive reinforcers are something a person likes and will work for such as food, toys or access to an animal.

Reinforcer Sampling   Also known as reinforcer assessment. A procedure where the reinforcers of a person (or animal) are determined in a systematic fashion.

Remedial Riding   Therapeutic horseback riding where goals and objectives are incorporated into the riding program.

Rescue League   An organized group that removes animals from undesirable situations or from shelters that cannot keep them. Animals are placed in new homes and, in some cases, prior to placement, basic training and/or medical care are provided.

Responsible Breeder   A responsible breeder is a person who breeds animals for the purpose of improving the breed. Responsible breeders are well-educated about their breeds and they care about the future of the animals they place. Responsible breeders adhere to ethical standards.

Responsible Pet Ownership   Engaging in responsible practices related to pet ownership, such as properly confining (e.g., leash, fence) and controlling one's pet at all times, providing routine veterinary care and exercise, providing pets with quality time and playtime, providing good nutrition through proper diet and clean water, cleaning up after one's pet and never letting a pet infringe on the rights of others.

Responsible Pet Ownership Neighborhood   A model where neighborhood associations take responsibility for ensuring that owners abide by responsible pet ownership guidelines. The model exists in neighborhoods, apartment complexes and mobile home parks.

Seizure Detection Dogs   Dogs that are used to signal an owner that seizures are about to occur. Some dogs have the natural ability to detect seizures; to date, this is not a skill that has been trained in dogs.

Smith, Elaine   Founder of Therapy Dogs International (TDI). The first TDI visits were in 1976.

Standards   A model of behavior that is generally accepted and adhered to; there are standards for particular areas such as animal-assisted therapy.

St. John Ambulance Therapy Dogs   Begun in Canada in 1992 as a therapy dog program, this group is a part of St. John's Ambulance, a charity that is 1,000 years old.

Stress   Mental or physical tension or strain. Both people and animals experience stress and therapy settings may be stressful for both volunteers and their animals.

Task Analysis   Breaking a task into smaller units of behavior. In therapy settings, it may be necessary to teach smaller parts of a task to someone who has learning problems. The task analytic approach can also be applied to animal training.

Therapeutic Riding   Involves horseback riding in therapy settings. Therapeutic riding can be an adapted recreational sport, remedial riding or hippotherapy.

Therapy Dogs Incorporated   An animal-assisted therapy group that registers owners and dog teams. The group was started in 1990 by Jack and Ann Butrick in Cheyenne, Wyoming.

Therapy Dogs International   An animal-assisted therapy group that registers owners and therapy dog teams. The group was started by Elaine Smith in 1976. TDI is based in Mendham, New Jersey.

Treatment Plan   In therapy settings, a treatment plan identifies the current status of individual clients and lists goals and objectives for specific treatment areas such as physical therapy, recreation therapy, etc. In different settings, a treatment plan may be called something else such as a Habilitation Plan, Individualized Educational Plan (IEP), etc.

Volunteer   A person who provides a service for no compensation.

York Retreat   An early AAT program in Yorkshire, England. Founded in the 1790s by the Society of Friends, this program incorporated animals into therapy programs.

Index

205

Index of Case Studies